Pick of the Crop, Two

Favorites from the Mississippi Delta

Published by
North Sunflower Academy PTA
148 Academy Road
Drew, Mississippi 38737
(601) 756-0088
(800) 208-4098

By North Sunflower Academy PTA

Additional copies may be obtained at the cost of $18.95,
plus $4.00 postage and handling, each book.

Mississippi residents add applicable sales tax.

Send to:
Pick of the Crop, Two
148 Academy Road
Drew, MS 38737
(601) 756-0088
(800) 208-4098
FAX (601) 756-2580
E-mail: nsa@tecinfo.com

First Printing   November, 1998   5,000 Copies
Second Printing   January, 1999   7,000 Copies

Barry McWilliams, a native Deltan and graduate of Mississippi State University with a degree in Art Education, has taught art at North Sunflower Academy for eight years. She is well-known in the area for her paintings in water color and her drawings in pen and ink.

ISBN #0-9666954-0-2

Printed in the USA by
WIMMER
The Wimmer Companies
Memphis
1-800-548-2537

FOREWORD

Homeward bound from some foreign strand, I stagger into Memphis airport, stubbled of chin and bloodshot of eye. Sour humored though I be, the Delta begins to work its magic the instant I hear those soft feminine accents spoken nowhere but between Memphis and Vicksburg. I search for the speakers and there they are—Delta women en route somewhere, cool, graceful, chic as even the Parisienne could never manage in this climate. I am almost home.

On the drive across the Delta, it is spring. Around oxbow lakes, wood ducks flash through cypress brakes seeking nesting sites. Fat cows graze in pastures yellow-carpeted with wild ranunculus. A shower cracks the earth's crust, and cotton sprouts burst through for the first touch of the hot Delta sun. Soybean seedlings draw emerald streaks across brown fields flat as a pool table. The pale green of rice just burst from seed dusts serpentine levees that writhe across fields fresh torn from lowland woods.

If I am lucky enough to spend the summer home, I join the Delta planter in watching the sky for needed rains, because I too work that incredibly fertile soil. While my writing colleagues at their expense account luncheons eat the eternal coq au vin with vegetables that have been traveling for a week across the continent, I carry up from the garden eggplant fruit gleaming like amethysts, tomatoes with the acid bite of new wine, lettuce that snaps under the fingernail like a chip of frozen butter, sprigs of aromatic rosemary and basil and, above all, the garden prize that no city dweller will ever know—sweet corn still in the milk stage rushed from stalk to boiling pot in 30 seconds.

On the first day of dove season, half the Delta's males disappear from normal haunts; on the first day of deer hunting, only the lame and halt remain at their job. Frost withers tomato vines, but brings rich flavor to mustard and turnip greens. Freezers begin to fill for the festive winter.

Then one afternoon I am working my garden and my heart leaps up, for overhead I hear that ragged gabbling that calls to the nomad deep inside every man. A skein of wild geese passes over, and my soul goes with them, captive of their same mindless wanderlust.

Weeks later seated at a sidewalk table sipping a syrupy aperitif, I ache because I am missing the sweet pleasures of the Delta winter. I miss those parties thrown together on the most preposterous pretexts—say, for instance, a Too-Much-Rain Party or a Drouth Party, or a We-Lost-to-Arkansas-but-wait till Next-Week-Party. I miss flirting with the beautiful women who understand that game superbly well and rarely let it get out of control. I miss talking weather and crops with the men.

Most of all, I miss the special civilization that Delta women have brought to what was only a few generations back a malaria-rotten swamp too hostile even for Choctaws. I miss going to the buffet sideboard and heaping a plate with venison simmered in wine spooned over Delta long grain rice, candied yams, okra and tomato stew. Try to order that kind of fare at La Tour d'Argent.

After only a few sessions of self-exiled brooding, there I am again at Memphis airport, wrinkled, with bloodshot eyes, groggy, but intoxicated with the cool beauty of Delta girls, for it means that just 12 miles down the road the Delta begins and I am almost home again.

Bern Keating
Greenville, Mississippi

3

Pick of the Crop, Two
Committee

Chairman
Becky Tollison

Co-Chairman
Brenda Vanlandingham

Editor and Typing Chairman
Kathryn Purcell

Artist
Barry McWilliams

Sustaining Advisors
Ann Grittman
Ruth Miller

Testing Chairman
Ann Elizabeth Arant

Steering Committee
Johnny McWilliams, Chairman

Valrie Blackwood	Tucker Miller
Ann Grittman	George Purcell
Ann Maxwell	Becky Tollison

PTA President

Foreword
Bern Keating

4

TABLE OF CONTENTS

Appetizers

and

Beverages

B. McWilliams

Dried Beef Cheese Ball

3 8-ounce packages cream
cheese, softened
1 2¼-ounce can ripe
olives, drained and
chopped
1 4-ounce can mushrooms,
drained and chopped
1 3-ounce jar dried beef,
chopped
1 bunch green onions,
chopped
1 tablespoon Accent
1 cup chopped pecans
Shredded parsley

• Combine cream cheese,
olives, mushrooms, dried
beef, green onions, and
Accent, mixing well.
• Shape into 2 or 3 balls; roll in
chopped pecans and parsley.
Chill. Serve with crackers.

Yield: 2 or 3 cheese balls

Cheese Nut Rounds

½ pound (2 sticks) butter,
softened
1 pound sharp Cheddar
cheese, grated
2 cups wheat flour
2 cups finely chopped nuts
1 teaspoon salt
1 teaspoon ground red
pepper

• Cream butter and cheese
using mixer. Add remaining
ingredients and mix. Shape
into three rolls, wrap in wax
paper, and chill thoroughly.
• Preheat oven to 325 degrees.
• Slice thinly, and place on
lightly greased cookie sheet.
• Bake 20 minutes, or until
edges begin to brown.

Yield: 10 dozen

Note: May be frozen and baked later.

Spinach Cheese Ball

2 8-ounce packages cream
  cheese, softened
3 green onions, finely
  chopped
4 ounces frozen spinach,
  squeezed dry
1 cup grated Cheddar
  cheese
1 8-ounce can water
  chestnuts, finely
  chopped
1 10-ounce package deli
  beef, finely chopped
⅛ teaspoon garlic powder
⅛ teaspoon seasoned salt
1 teaspoon Worcestershire
  sauce

• Mix all ingredients in large
  mixing bowl. Shape into
  1 large ball or 2 small balls.
  Serve with crackers.

Yield: 30 appetizer servings

Marinated Cheese

½ cup olive oil
½ cup white wine vinegar
1 2-ounce jar diced
  pimiento, drained
3 tablespoons fresh
  parsley, chopped
3 tablespoons green
  onions, minced
3 cloves garlic, minced
1 teaspoon sugar
¾ teaspoon dried whole
  basil
½ teaspoon salt
½ teaspoon freshly ground
  black pepper
1 8-ounce package sharp
  Cheddar cheese, chilled
1 8-ounce package cream
  cheese, chilled
Fresh parsley sprigs

- Combine olive oil, vinegar, pimiento, parsley, green onion, garlic, sugar, basil, salt, and black pepper in a jar; cover tightly, and shake vigorously. Set marinade mixture aside.

- Cut block of Cheddar cheese into ¼-inch-thick slices; set aside. Repeat procedure with cream cheese. Arrange cheese slices alternately in a shallow baking dish, standing slices on edge. Pour marinade over cheese slices. Cover and marinate in refrigerator at least 8 hours.

- Transfer cheese slices to a serving platter in the same alternating fashion, reserving marinade. Let marinade come to room temperature and spoon marinade over cheese slices. Garnish with fresh parsley. Serve with assorted crackers.

Yield: 16 appetizer servings

Brie Wrapped in Phyllo

12 sheets frozen phyllo pastry, thawed
Butter-flavored cooking spray
1 2-pound round Brie cheese
¼ cup honey
1 cup sliced almonds
¾ cup brown sugar

- Preheat oven to 350 degrees.
- Place 1 sheet of phyllo on a baking sheet coated with cooking spray. (Keep remaining pastry covered with a slightly damp towel to prevent it from drying out.) Coat pastry on baking sheet with cooking spray. Layer 5 additional pastry sheets on top, coating each with cooking spray.
- Remove and discard rind from Brie; place Brie on stacked sheets and cover with honey, sliced almonds, and brown sugar. Bring edges of pastry up over cheese. Layer remaining 6 pastry sheets, spraying each; place over Brie, tucking edges under. Bake 30 minutes or until golden. Let stand at least 30 minutes before serving.

Yield: 24 to 30 servings

Guacamole Dip

3 ripe avocados
3 tomatoes, finely chopped
2 green onions, chopped
½ clove garlic, pressed
3 tablespoons olive oil
1 tablespoon mayonnaise
Salt
Ground red pepper
Chili powder
Cumin
Lemon juice

• Peel, pit, and mash avocados with fork. Blend with tomato, green onion, garlic, oil, and mayonnaise. Add salt, red pepper, chili powder, cumin, and lemon juice to taste. Serve with tortilla chips.

Yield: 3 cups

Sunshine Fruit Dip

4 cups sugar
8 tablespoons all-purpose flour
8 eggs, whisked
1 cup lemon juice
2 cups orange juice
2 cups pineapple juice

• Mix sugar and flour together in saucepan; add eggs. Blend well. Add fruit juices and cook over low heat until mixture barely starts to thicken.
• Cool and serve with fresh fruit.

Yield: 2 quarts

Note: Keeps 2 to 3 weeks in refrigerator.

Sausage Mushroom Spread

8 ounces fresh mushrooms, finely chopped
2 teaspoons olive oil
½ pound ground sausage
3 green onions, finely chopped
2 teaspoons crushed red pepper
4 ounces cream cheese, softened
4 ounces sour cream
1 ounce bleu cheese
¼ cup mayonnaise

• Sauté mushrooms in olive oil until dark; drain. Cook sausage and drain.

• Combine all ingredients. Refrigerate for 4 to 24 hours. Serve with toast rounds.

Yield: 3 cups

Baked Onion Spread

3 cups chopped onion
3 8-ounce packages cream cheese, softened
2 cups Parmesan cheese
½ cup mayonnaise

• Preheat oven to 425 degrees.

• Combine all ingredients. Place into ovenproof dish.

• Bake 15 minutes. Serve warm with crackers.

Yield: 2 quarts

Parmesan-Spinach Spread

1 10-ounce package
  frozen chopped spinach,
  thawed
1¼ cups freshly grated
  Parmesan cheese,
  divided
1 14-ounce can artichoke
  hearts, drained and
  chopped
¼ cup finely chopped
  onion
1 cup grated mozzarella
  cheese
¾ cup mayonnaise or
  salad dressing
1 teaspoon hot sauce
1 teaspoon dried Italian
  seasoning
½ teaspoon garlic powder
¼ teaspoon freshly ground
  black pepper
1 teaspoon paprika

• Preheat oven to 350 degrees.
• Press spinach between paper towels to remove excess moisture.
• Combine spinach, 1 cup of the Parmesan cheese, the artichokes, onion, mozzarella cheese, mayonnaise, hot sauce, Italian seasoning, garlic powder, and black pepper. Spoon into a greased 1-quart baking dish.
• Bake 10 minutes. Sprinkle with the remaining ¼ cup Parmesan cheese and paprika. Bake an additional 10 minutes. Serve with crackers or party rye.

Yield: 4 cups

Cucumber Sandwiches

3 large cucumbers, peeled
   and sliced
2 tablespoons white
   vinegar
Cold water
1 8-ounce package cream
   cheese, softened
1 tablespoon Italian salad
   dressing mix
2 tablespoons milk
1 loaf wheat or white
   bread, cut in 2-inch
   rounds
Paprika

• Wash, peel, and slice
  cucumbers. Place cucumber
  slices in a medium bowl; add
  vinegar and enough cold
  water to cover. Refrigerate
  cucumbers at least 1 hour.

• Combine cream cheese,
  Italian salad dressing mix,
  and milk, mixing well.

• Drain cucumbers on paper
  towels.

• Spread cream cheese mixture evenly on bread rounds;
  top with a cucumber slice,
  and sprinkle with paprika.

• Refrigerate sandwiches in an
  airtight container at least
  1 hour before serving.

Yield: 40 open face sandwiches

Cajun Smoked Catfish Spread

1 8-ounce package cream cheese, softened
3 tablespoons mayonnaise
3 tablespoons whipping cream
2 tablespoons chopped fresh parsley
¾ cup chopped green onions
¾ cup chopped pimiento
1 tablespoon grated onion
3 garlic cloves, chopped
½ teaspoon Worcestershire sauce
1 tablespoon sherry
2 dashes hot sauce
Salt
Red pepper
Lemon juice
4 7-ounce smoked catfish fillets, chopped (recipe follows)

- In a mixing bowl, combine cream cheese, mayonnaise, and cream. Add parsley, green onion, pimiento, onion, garlic, Worcestershire sauce, sherry, and hot sauce, mixing well.
- Stir in salt, pepper, and lemon juice to taste. Fold in smoked catfish fillets. Serve with crackers or toast points.

Yield: 30 appetizer servings

Smoked Catfish

4 7-ounce catfish fillets
¾ cup sherry
¾ cup lemon juice
½ pound (2 sticks) butter, melted
1 tablespoon salt
1 tablespoon red pepper
Dash of hot sauce
1 teaspoon powdered thyme

- Combine sherry, lemon juice, butter, salt, red pepper, hot sauce, and thyme. Marinate fish fillets in this mixture for 45 minutes, turning once.
- Set up smoker and place fillets on grill. Smoke 1 hour.

Fresh Vegetable Dill Dip

1 cup sour cream
1 cup mayonnaise
1 tablespoon finely
chopped green onions
1 tablespoon chopped
parsley
1 tablespoon dill weed
1 tablespoon Bon Appetit
seasoning

• Mix all ingredients; cover
tightly and refrigerate overnight. Serve with assorted
fresh vegetables.

Yield: 2 cups

Ham and Cheese Dip

1 loaf French bread
1½ cups sour cream
2 cups grated Cheddar
cheese
1 8-ounce package cream
cheese, softened
⅓ cup chopped green
onion
½ cup chopped ham
Dash of Worcestershire
sauce

• Preheat oven to 350 degrees.
• Slice off top of bread and
hollow out inside.
• Mix remaining ingredients.
Pour into loaf. Replace bread
top. Wrap in foil.
• Bake 1 hour. Use pieces of
bread from hollowed-out loaf
for dipping or use crackers.

Yield: 25 appetizer servings

17

Mexican Dip

1 pound processed cheese loaf, cubed
2 6-ounce rolls garlic cheese
1 15-ounce can chili without beans
1 15-ounce can tamales
1 11½-ounce jar prepared salsa
Jalapeño slices

- Place cheese in microwave-proof bowl. Add chili and tamales. Heat on medium power until cheese is partially melted and tamales have softened.
- Add salsa and jalapeño slices. Mix together and heat thoroughly. Serve hot with tortilla chips.

Yield: 2½ quarts

Note: To cook in slow cooker, heat on high for 1¹/₂ hours.

Spinach Dip

1 10-ounce package chopped spinach
⅓ cup chopped parsley
⅓ cup chopped green onions
1 tablespoon dehydrated onion
½ teaspoon black pepper
½ teaspoon salt
1 cup mayonnaise
1 tablespoon lemon juice

- Cook spinach according to package directions. Drain well.
- Mix all ingredients in order listed. Refrigerate 1 hour before serving. Serve with toast rounds.

Yield: 3 cups

Note: Can also be used as a sandwich spread.

Catfish Nuggets with Bleu Cheese-Sour Cream Dip

2 pounds catfish fillets
1 cup finely crushed round cheese crackers
½ cup grated Parmesan cheese
¼ cup sesame seeds
½ teaspoon salt
¼ teaspoon pepper
¼ pound (1 stick) butter, melted

- Preheat oven to 400 degrees.
- Cut fillets into one-inch cubes and set aside.
- Combine cracker crumbs, cheese, sesame seeds, salt and pepper in a small bowl. Dip fish cubes in butter and roll in cracker crumbs. Place fish ½ inch apart on aluminum foil lined baking sheets.
- Bake, uncovered, 20 minutes, or until fish is golden brown. Serve immediately with Bleu Cheese Sour Cream Dip.

Yield: 40 nuggets

Bleu Cheese Sour Cream Dip

1 8-ounce carton sour cream
2 tablespoons crumbled bleu cheese
¼ cup finely minced onion
¼ teaspoon salt
Fresh chopped parsley, optional

- Combine sour cream, bleu cheese, onion, and salt. Refrigerate until ready to serve. Garnish with fresh parsley, if desired.

Yield: 1½ cups

Shrimp in Sour Cream Dip

**1 pound shrimp, cooked
and peeled
1 4-ounce can sliced
mushrooms, drained
2 tablespoons chopped
green onions
2 tablespoons butter
1 tablespoon all-purpose
flour
1 10-ounce can cream of
shrimp soup
1 cup sour cream
Dash of pepper**

- If shrimp are large, cut in half.
- Sauté mushrooms and onions in butter over medium heat until onions are tender. Blend in flour. Add soup, and cook until thickened, stirring constantly.
- Add sour cream, pepper, and shrimp. Heat thoroughly. Serve with toast points.

Yield: 5 cups

Variation: Canned shrimp can be substituted. Drain and rinse before using.

Toast Points

**1 loaf bread
¼ pound (1 stick) butter**

- Preheat oven to 200 degrees.
- Melt butter. Cut bread slices into desired shapes. Brush butter on both sides of bread using a pastry brush. Place on baking sheet.
- Bake 1 hour.

Crabmeat Mornay

1 small bunch green onions,
chopped
½ cup fresh parsley,
chopped
¼ pound (1 stick) butter
2 tablespoons all-purpose
flour
¾ pint half-and-half
¾ pound grated Swiss
cheese
Ground red pepper
Tabasco
Salt
1 pound fresh lump
crabmeat
1 tablespoon dry sherry

- In a heavy saucepan, sauté onions and parsley in butter. Blend in flour; add half-and-half, stirring constantly. Add cheese and continue stirring until cheese melts. Blend in red pepper, Tabasco, and salt. Gently fold in crabmeat.
- Just before serving, add sherry. Serve in a chafing dish with toast rounds or in patty shells.

Yield: 30 appetizer servings

Smoked Oysters

Worcestershire sauce
2 cans smoked oysters,
drained
1 8-ounce can sliced water
chestnuts, drained
Bacon, cut into 2½-inch
strips

- Put a drop of Worcestershire sauce on each oyster. Wrap 1 oyster and 1 water chestnut slice with a strip of bacon. Secure with a wooden pick. Repeat until all oysters have been wrapped.
- Sauté in a non-stick skillet until bacon is browned on all sides. Place on a paper towel to drain.

Yield: about 30

Note: These can be cooked on the grill, refrigerated, then reheated in non-stick skillet just before serving.

21

Salmon Mousse with Dill Sauce

1 envelope unflavored
  gelatin
¼ cup water, room
  temperature
¼ cup water, boiling
½ medium onion, sliced
2 tablespoons lemon juice
1 to 2 teaspoons dill seed,
  ground
½ teaspoon paprika
½ teaspoon salt
½ teaspoon black pepper
1 teaspoon horseradish
1 teaspoon Tabasco
1 8-ounce package cream
  cheese, softened
¼ cup mayonnaise
Red food coloring
1 small package smoked
  salmon, optional
1 1-pound can pink salmon,
  best quality
¼ teaspoon liquid smoke
Garnish: Stuffed green
  olives, pitted black olives,
  cucumbers, leaf lettuce,
  lemons

- Sprinkle gelatin over ¼ cup water at room temperature. Add ¼ cup boiling water and stir until gelatin is dissolved. Blend with onion and lemon juice.

- Blend in dill seed, paprika, salt, black pepper, horseradish, and Tabasco. Add cream cheese and mayonnaise and stir until smooth. Carefully add a few drops red food coloring.

- If using smoked salmon, blend it in next until texture disappears. Discard bones and skin from canned salmon and add along with liquid smoke.

- Place in greased fish mold. Refrigerate until completely set.

- Unmold onto leaf lettuce; garnish with a slice of stuffed green olive for eye, slices of pitted black olives cut in half into semicircles for scales, or score unpeeled cucumbers and slice thinly, cut in half horizontally, overlap for scales. Surround with Dill Sauce. Arrange thinly sliced lemons at bottom of platter (below salmon's tummy) for additional color.

Yield: 50 appetizer servings

22

Note: One recipe will fill a standard lucite fish mold but is not enough for a large metal mold. To double recipe, prepare twice and combine at end.

Dill Sauce

1 teaspoon salt
¼ teaspoon white pepper
2 cups sour cream
3 tablespoons finely chopped dill weed
¼ cup fresh lemon juice or grated rind of one lemon

• If planning to serve the mousse as a first course with sauce on the side, combine ingredients, using the lemon juice, and refrigerate several hours.

• To serve the mousse as an hors d'oeuvre, drain excess liquid from sour cream and use the lemon rind. This will make a slightly thicker sauce to outline the fish shape.

Crabmeat Mousse

1 envelope unflavored
gelatin
3 tablespoons cold water
¼ cup mayonnaise
2 tablespoons lemon juice
4 tablespoons lime juice,
divided
2 tablespoons chopped
chives, divided
1 tablespoon chopped
fresh parsley
1 tablespoon prepared
mustard
¼ teaspoon salt
¼ teaspoon pepper
2 cups fresh lump
crabmeat
¾ cup whipping cream,
whipped
3 limes, thinly sliced
2 avocados, peeled and
mashed

• Sprinkle gelatin over cold
water, let stand 1 minute.
Cook over low heat, stirring
until gelatin dissolves, about 2
minutes.

• Combine gelatin mixture,
mayonnaise, lemon juice,
2 tablespoons of the lime
juice, 1 tablespoon of the
chives, parsley, mustard, salt,
and pepper in a large mixing
bowl. Fold in crabmeat and
whipped cream; spoon into
a lightly greased 4-cup ring
mold.

• Cover and chill until set.
Unmold onto a serving plate.
Arrange thin lime slices
around the edge.

• Combine avocado and the
remaining 2 tablespoons lime
juice; spoon into center of
mousse, and sprinkle with the
remaining 1 tablespoon
chives. Serve with assorted
crackers.

Yield: 20 to 25 appetizer servings

Crab-Stuffed Mushrooms

1½ pounds very large
fresh mushrooms,
about 18
½ cup chopped onion
1 garlic clove, minced
5 tablespoons butter,
divided
½ cup soft bread crumbs
¼ cup chopped fresh
parsley
2 tablespoons dry sherry
½ teaspoon Worcestershire
sauce
½ teaspoon salt
¼ teaspoon red pepper
¼ cup mayonnaise
2 tablespoons grated
Parmesan cheese
8 ounces fresh lump
crabmeat

- Preheat oven to 350 degrees.
- Remove and chop mushroom stems; set mushroom caps aside.
- Sauté chopped mushroom stems, onion, and garlic in 3 tablespoons of the butter until tender.
- Remove from heat. Stir in bread crumbs, parsley, sherry, Worcestershire sauce, salt, red pepper, mayonnaise, and Parmesan cheese until well blended. Gently fold in crabmeat.
- Spoon crabmeat mixture evenly into mushroom caps; place on a rack in a broiler pan. Drizzle with the remaining 2 tablespoons butter.
- Bake 20 minutes.

Yield: 18 mushrooms

Mushroom Cheese Stromboli

¼ pound fresh mushrooms
1 tablespoon butter
1 1-pound loaf frozen
bread dough, thawed
3 ounces thinly sliced
pepperoni
6 ounces thinly sliced
mozzarella cheese
4 ounces thinly sliced
Provolone cheese
1 cup grated Parmesan
cheese
⅓ cup spaghetti sauce
1 tablespoon dried parsley
flakes
½ teaspoon dried oregano
1 egg yolk
½ teaspoon water
Additional Parmesan
cheese, optional

- Preheat oven to 350 degrees.
- Sauté mushrooms in butter until tender.
- On a lightly floured board, roll dough into a 30-inch by 8-inch rectangle; cut into two 15-inch by 8-inch pieces.
- On the long side of each piece, layer pepperoni, cheeses, mushrooms, spaghetti sauce, parsley and oregano. Fold over dough and pinch to seal.
- Combine egg and water; brush over edges and ends of dough.
- Cut five small steam vents in the top of each roll with a sharp knife. Place on greased baking sheets. Sprinkle with Parmesan cheese, if desired.
- Bake 30 minutes or until golden brown. Slice and serve warm.

Yield: 36 slices

Note: Baked stromboli can be frozen for up to 1 month.

Sausage Bites with Mustard

1 16-ounce package
  smoked sausage
Maple syrup
Coarsely ground black
  pepper

- Cover sausage with syrup; coat with coarsely ground black pepper.
- Bake at 350 degrees 30 to 45 minutes.
- For serving, cut into bite-size pieces and dip into mustard sauce.

Yield: 16 appetizer servings

Mustard Sauce

1 4-ounce can dry mustard
1 cup white vinegar
1 cup sugar
2 egg yolks, beaten
¾ cup prepared mustard
1½ cups salad dressing

- Mix dry mustard and vinegar. Cover and let sit overnight.
- In a double boiler, combine mustard and vinegar mixture, sugar, and beaten egg yolks. Cook until thick, stirring occasionally.
- Stir in prepared mustard and salad dressing, stirring to blend.

Zesty Sausage Squares

1 pound ground hot
  sausage
½ cup chopped onion
⅔ cup milk
1 egg
2 cups biscuit baking mix
1 cup grated sharp
  Cheddar cheese
½ cup grated Parmesan
  cheese
¼ cup sour cream
2 tablespoons chopped
  parsley
2 cloves garlic, finely
  minced

- Preheat oven to 350 degrees.
- Sauté sausage and onion in skillet until sausage is browned and onion is tender. Drain and set aside.
- Combine milk and egg, beating well. Stir in remaining ingredients until thoroughly mixed. Add sausage-onion mixture.
- Spread into a greased 9 by 13-inch baking dish.
- Bake 25 minutes, or until golden brown. Cut into bite-size squares. Serve immediately.

Yield: 48 squares.

Bacon Roll Ups

4 tablespoons butter
½ cup water
1½ cups herb seasoned
stuffing
1 egg, beaten
¼ pound ground hot
sausage
¾ pound bacon slices, cut
into thirds

• Heat butter and water until butter is melted. Combine with stuffing, add egg and sausage. Mix thoroughly. Chill 30 minutes.

• Shape into small cocoons, about the size of a pecan. Wrap bacon slices around cocoons, fasten with a wooden pick.

• For oven baking, preheat oven to 375 degrees. Bake in a shallow pan 35 minutes, or until crisp on all sides. Drain and serve immediately.

• For microwave, place ½ of the cocoons on a paper towel-lined glass dish; microwave on high 8 minutes, or until bacon is browned and crisp. Blot with paper towels and serve hot.

Yield: 25 to 30 appetizers

Chicken Marmalade

4 chicken breast halves
¼ cup orange marmalade
2 tablespoons soy sauce
1 tablespoon lemon juice
½ teaspoon salt
½ teaspoon ginger
½ teaspoon garlic powder
1 16-ounce package thin
sliced bacon

- Remove skin and bones from chicken. Cut into bite size pieces and place in shallow pan.
- Combine marmalade, soy sauce, lemon juice, and seasonings. Pour over chicken to marinate 1 hour. Drain, reserving marinade.
- Broil bacon until partially cooked, but not crisp. Cut each slice in half, wrap around chicken pieces, and secure with wooden pick.
- Broil 5 to 6 minutes, basting with marinade, until chicken is tender and bacon is crisp. Turn to broil all sides evenly.

Yield: 2 dozen

Hawaiian Meatballs

1½ pounds ground beef
¾ cup quick oats
1 8-ounce can water
  chestnuts, drained and
  chopped
1 tablespoon Accent
½ teaspoon onion salt
½ teaspoon garlic powder
¼ teaspoon salt
1 tablespoon soy sauce
⅛ teaspoon Tabasco
1 egg
½ cup milk

- Preheat oven to 350 degrees.
- Combine all ingredients.
  Shape into small meatballs.
- Bake for 20 minutes, or until
  browned; cool. (Meatballs can
  be frozen at this point.) Prior
  to serving, combine meatballs
  and Sauce; heat thoroughly.
  Serve in a chafing dish.

Yield: 60 meatballs

Sauce

1 cup brown sugar, firmly
  packed
2 tablespoons cornstarch
1 8½-ounce can crushed
  pineapple, drained;
  reserve juice
1 cup beef bouillon or
  broth
½ cup vinegar
2 teaspoons soy sauce
¾ cup chopped green
  pepper

- Combine sugar and corn-
  starch in a saucepan. Add
  pineapple juice, bouillon or
  broth, vinegar, and soy
  sauce.
- Bring to a boil, stirring
  constantly for 1 minute.
  Blend in pineapple and
  green pepper.

Note: If short on time, purchase meatballs and use Sauce.

Hot and Spicy Meatballs

¾ **pound ground beef**
¾ **cup fine bread crumbs**
¾ **teaspoon salt**
½ **teaspoon pepper**
½ **teaspoon Accent**
1½ **tablespoons minced onion**
½ **teaspoon horseradish**
3 **drops Tabasco**
2 **eggs, beaten**
1 **tablespoon butter**

• Combine ground beef, bread crumbs, salt, pepper, Accent, onion, horseradish, Tabasco, and eggs. Mix well.

• Shape into balls. Sauté in a skillet with the butter until browned; remove and drain.

• Pour off pan drippings. Return meatballs to skillet; pour Sauce over meatballs. Simmer 10 minutes. Serve hot.

Yield: 40 meatballs

Sauce

¾ **cup ketchup**
½ **cup water**
¼ **cup cider vinegar**
2 **tablespoons brown sugar**
1 **tablespoon minced onion**
2 **teaspoons Worcestershire sauce**
1½ **teaspoons salt**
1 **teaspoon dry mustard**
¼ **teaspoon pepper**
3 **drops Tabasco**
Pinch of cayenne pepper

• Combine all ingredients in saucepan; heat over low heat until blended.

Artichoke Squares

1 6-ounce jar marinated
   artichokes
1 14-ounce can plain
   artichokes, drained
1 small onion, finely
   chopped
1 clove garlic, minced
4 eggs, beaten
¼ cup fine bread crumbs
¼ teaspoon salt
⅛ teaspoon oregano
¼ teaspoon Tabasco
½ pound sharp Cheddar
   cheese, grated
2 teaspoons parsley

- Preheat oven to 325 degrees.
- Drain artichoke marinade into skillet; discard plain juice. Chop all artichokes into small pieces; set aside.
- Add onion and garlic to skillet; sauté until onion is clear. Add eggs, bread crumbs, and seasonings. Stir in Tabasco, cheese, parsley, artichokes, and onion mixture. Pour into a greased 8 by 8-inch baking dish.
- Bake 30 minutes. Allow to cool in pan. Cut into 1-inch squares.

Yield: 64 squares

Note: Freezes well.

Pepperoni Pizza Spread

8 ounces cream cheese, softened
½ cup sour cream
1 teaspoon dried, crushed oregano
⅛ teaspoon garlic powder
⅛ teaspoon crushed red pepper, optional
1 cup pizza sauce
½ cup chopped pepperoni
¼ cup sliced green onion
¼ cup chopped bell pepper
½ cup grated mozzarella cheese

- Preheat oven to 350 degrees.
- Combine cream cheese, sour cream, oregano, garlic powder, and red pepper, if desired. Spread evenly in 9 or 10-inch quiche dish or pie pan. Spread pizza sauce over top. Sprinkle with pepperoni, green onion, and bell pepper.
- Bake 10 minutes. Top with mozzarella cheese. Bake an additional 5 minutes, or until cheese is melted. Serve with crackers.

Yield: 16 to 20 appetizer servings

Mexican Cheese Squares

1 12-ounce can evaporated milk
2 eggs, beaten
2 4-ounce cans chopped green chilies, drained, reserving juice
1 cup all-purpose flour
1 pound Cheddar cheese, grated
1 pound Monterey Jack cheese with jalapeño peppers, grated

- Preheat oven to 350 degrees.
- In blender, mix evaporated milk, eggs, and juice from chilies; blend in flour.
- Put grated cheese in greased 9 by 13- inch baking dish. Top with chopped chilies. Pour milk mixture over the cheese and chilies. Bake 30 to 35 minutes or until brown. Cool; slice into squares.

Yield: 48 squares

Fajita Grilled Shrimp

**1½ pounds large shrimp,
 peeled
2 tablespoons brown sugar
1½ teaspoons chili powder
1 teaspoon fajita dry spice
Thick-sliced bacon, cut
 into fourths**

• Combine shrimp with brown sugar, chili powder, and dry spice. Refrigerate for 1 to 2 hours.

• Wrap each shrimp with bacon and secure with wooden pick. Return to marinade for 5 to 10 minutes. Grill over hot coals until bacon is crisp.

Yield: 6 to 8 servings

Stuffed Banana Peppers

**1 pound ground pork
 sausage, cooked and
 drained
1 9-ounce can bean dip
1 3-ounce package cream
 cheese, softened
1 clove garlic, crushed
1 tablespoon prepared
 mustard
Dash of Tabasco
1 teaspoon Worcestershire
 sauce
Fresh banana peppers**

• Combine sausage, bean dip, cream cheese, garlic, mustard, Tabasco, and Worcestershire sauce.

• Slice peppers in half lengthwise and seed; stuff with sausage mixture. Chill.

Yield: 30 appetizers

Note: Filling will freeze for later use. Do not freeze stuffed peppers.

35

Mexican Cheesecake

1 cup ground corn chips,
  processed to the
  consistency of coarse
  meal
2 tablespoons unsalted
  butter, melted
4 tablespoons all-purpose
  flour
1 pound light cream
  cheese, softened
2 cups low-fat yogurt
  cheese (recipe follows)
4 large eggs
1 teaspoon dried oregano
1½ teaspoons cumin
½ teaspoon garlic powder
1 teaspoon chili powder
½ teaspoon freshly ground
  black pepper
½ teaspoon ground
  cayenne pepper
¼ teaspoon salt

- Preheat oven to 350 degrees.
- Combine corn chips, butter, and flour in a greased 9-inch springform pan. Mix well and pat onto the bottom of the pan. Place on center shelf of the oven and bake about 10 minutes. Remove from oven.
- In a large mixing bowl, combine cheeses; beat on medium speed until smooth. Add eggs, one at a time, mixing well. Add oregano, cumin, garlic powder, chili powder, black pepper, cayenne pepper, and salt. Mix 1 to 2 minutes more. Pour filling into prepared pan and spread evenly with a spatula.
- Bake on center shelf of oven 30 to 40 minutes, or until set. Remove from oven and cool. Cover and refrigerate. Cheesecake can be made 2 days in advance.
- To serve cheesecake, remove sides from springform pan and place cheesecake on a serving tray. Spread half the Salsa over top of cheesecake and place other half in a serving bowl.

Yield: one 9-inch cheesecake

(Continued on next page)

Mexican Cheesecake *(Continued)*

Salsa

**2 cups tomatoes, seeded,
chopped
2½ tablespoons fresh
jalapeño peppers,
seeded, chopped
½ cup green onions,
chopped
2 tablespoons fresh
cilantro, chopped
4 teaspoons garlic, peeled,
minced
2 tablespoons lime juice
Pinch of cayenne pepper
Salt
Black pepper**

• Mix all ingredients and allow
to stand for a few minutes,
letting flavors blend.

Yield: 3 cups

Low Fat Yogurt Cheese

**32 ounces low fat plain
yogurt, containing no
gelatin**

• Place the yogurt in a colander
lined with a coffee filter.
Cover with plastic wrap;
place in refrigerator for at
least 12 hours. Drain off
liquid. The solid mass is
yogurt cheese.

*Note: Garnish the cheesecake with tortilla chips. Guests can spread
a little cheesecake and salsa on a chip.*

Instant Coffee Blends

Vienna Blend

½ **cup instant coffee granules**
⅔ **cup sugar**
⅔ **cup powdered non-dairy coffee creamer**
½ **teaspoon ground cinnamon**

Orange Blend

½ **cup instant coffee granules**
¾ **cup sugar**
1 **cup powdered non-dairy coffee creamer**
½ **teaspoon dried orange peel**

Mocha Blend

½ **cup instant coffee granules**
¾ **cup sugar**
1 **cup powdered non-dairy coffee creamer**
2 **tablespoons cocoa**

• Combine all ingredients for each in container of electric blender; process until smooth, stopping once to scrape down sides, if necessary. For each serving, spoon 2 tablespoons coffee blend of your choice into an 8-ounce cup of boiling water.

Note: These blends can be stored in airtight containers at room temperature for several months.

Irish Cream for Coffee

1 14-ounce can sweetened
  condensed milk
1 cup whipping cream,
  whipped
1 cup Irish whiskey
2 tablespoons chocolate
  syrup

• Combine all ingredients, mixing well. Store in refrigerator and add to coffee according to taste.

Yield: 3¾ cups

Coffee Punch

1 quart strong coffee
5 tablespoons sugar
5 teaspoons vanilla extract
1 pint bourbon
½ gallon vanilla ice cream
1 pint whipping cream,
  whipped

• Cool coffee; add sugar and vanilla. Stir in bourbon and pour into punch bowl. Add ice cream and stir. Serve with whipped cream on top.

Yield: 24 cups

Hot Chocolate

1½ cups sugar
2 heaping tablespoons
  cocoa
2 cups water
1 gallon milk
1 12-ounce can
  evaporated milk
Marshmallows

- Combine sugar and cocoa in saucepan; add water. Boil until syrupy.
- Reduce heat to medium; add milk and evaporated milk.
- After thoroughly heated, serve topped with marshmallows.

Yield: 16 Servings

Note: Will keep in the refrigerator. Reheat when ready to serve.

Hot Spiced Tea

2 tablespoons allspice
1 stick cinnamon
1 tablespoon whole cloves
4 cups water
2 cups sugar
6 teabags
12 cups water
2 6-ounce cans frozen
  lemonade concentrate,
  undiluted
2 6-ounce cans frozen
  orange juice
  concentrate, undiluted

- Place allspice, cinnamon, and cloves in spice bag. Combine spices, 4 cups water, and 2 cups sugar in a saucepan; heat to boiling.
- Steep teabags in 12 cups water. Add sugar and spice mixture to tea, removing the spice bag; cool. Add lemonade and orange juice concentrates, stirring until blended.

Yield: 1 gallon

Festive Hot Tea

7 cups water
½ cup sugar
1 3-ounce box strawberry
  Jell-o
1 3-ounce box cherry Jell-o
2 cups pineapple juice
1½ cups orange juice
¼ cup lemon juice
1½ cups water
2 large tea bags
1 tablespoon whole cloves
3 cinnamon sticks
¼ teaspoon ginger

• Boil 7 cups water. Add
  sugar and stir until sugar is
  dissolved. Add and dissolve
  both boxes of Jell-o. Add all
  juices to Jell-o mixture.
• Boil 1½ cups water, tea
  bags, and spices for
  15 minutes; pour through
  strainer into Jell-o mixture.
  Serve hot.

Yield: 3 quarts

Summer Tea

4 cups boiling water
8 small tea bags
2 cups sugar
1 6-ounce can frozen
  orange juice concentrate,
  thawed
1 6-ounce can frozen
  lemonade concentrate,
  thawed

• Bring water to a boil.
  Remove from heat, add tea
  bags, steep for 20 minutes.
• Remove tea bags, add sugar
  and stir until dissolved.
• Pour into a gallon jug; add
  orange juice and lemonade.
  Add water to almost fill jug.

Yield: 1 gallon

Note: Put a sprig of fresh mint in each glass when serving.

Hot Tomato Drink

**1 46-ounce can tomato
juice
2 10½-ounce cans beef
consommé
1 soup can water
¼ teaspoon Tabasco
2 teaspoons
Worcestershire sauce
1 teaspoon prepared
mustard
2 tablespoons onion,
minced
2 tablespoons celery,
minced
2 tablespoons butter
Lemon slices, optional**

• Combine tomato juice,
consommé, water, Tabasco,
Worcestershire sauce, and
mustard in saucepan.

• Sauté onion and celery in
butter until tender; add to
juice mixture and bring to a
boil. Simmer 15 minutes.

• To serve, pour into mugs
and place lemon slice on
top, if desired.

Yield: 10 servings

Strawberry Punch

**2 10-ounce boxes frozen
strawberries, thawed
2 6-ounce cans frozen
orange juice
concentrate, undiluted
2 lemons, juiced
2 cups sugar
Red food coloring,
optional**

• Puree frozen berries in
blender with about 2 cups
of water.

• Combine all ingredients in a
gallon jug; fill with water.
Serve chilled.

Yield: 1 gallon

Party Punch

**1 3-ounce box strawberry
Jell-o
2 cups boiling water
1 cup sugar
4 cups cold water
1 6-ounce can frozen
lemonade concentrate
1 46-ounce can pineapple
juice
2 quarts ginger ale**

• Dissolve Jell-o in boiling
water; add sugar and stir until
dissolved. Add cold water and
lemonade; mix well. Pour in
pineapple juice.

• Freeze punch in a plastic
gallon container until slushy.
Add ginger ale when ready to
serve.

Yield: 1½ gallons

Tea Punch

8 oranges, divided
12 lemons, divided
3 cups sugar, divided
1½ gallons water
8 large tea bags
48 ounces Concord
   grape juice

- Slice 4 oranges and 6 lemons. Place in baking dish and sprinkle with 1 cup sugar; let sit for at least one hour, stirring occasionally.

- Juice remaining oranges and lemons; set aside.

- Make 1½ gallons strong tea by bringing water to a boil, decrease temperature to medium, and add tea bags. Steep for 30 minutes. While tea is still hot, add remaining 2 cups of sugar; stir to dissolve. Cool.

- Add grape juice, juice of oranges and lemons, and sliced fruit. Chill. Fruit may be discarded, eaten, or left to float in tea.

Yield: 2¼ gallons

Bloody Marys

46 ounces tomato juice
6 ounces spicy hot tomato
juice
½ cup lemon juice
½ cup Worcestershire
sauce
1 tablespoon salt
1 tablespoon prepared
mustard
Dash of Tabasco
1 cup vodka
Garnish: Celery sticks

• Combine all ingredients until
blended. Serve in glasses
garnished with celery sticks.

Yield: 2 quarts

Mimosa Hawaiian

1 12-ounce can apricot
nectar
1 12-ounce can pineapple
juice
1 6-ounce can frozen
orange juice
concentrate, undiluted
¾ cup water
1 fifth dry white
champagne, chilled

• Combine apricot nectar,
pineapple juice, orange juice
concentrate, and water in a
large pitcher; stir well. Chill.
Stir in champagne immedi-
ately before serving.

Yield: 6 servings

Frozen Margaritas

Fresh lime slices
Salt
1 6-ounce can frozen
  limeade, thawed
¾ cup tequila
¼ cup Triple Sec
Crushed ice

- Rub rim of glasses with fresh lime slice; place in salt. Set aside.
- Combine limeade, tequila, and Triple Sec in blender. Add enough crushed ice to fill ¾ full. Blend and serve in prepared glasses.

Yield: 1 quart

Brandy Alexander

⅓ cup brandy
⅓ cup creme de cacao
  liqueur
Vanilla ice cream
Nutmeg

- Pour brandy and liqueur into blender. Gradually add ice cream until blender is filled to 4 to 5 cups, blend until smooth.
- Serve in small glasses and sprinkle with nutmeg.

Yield: 8 servings

Brunch

B. McWilliams

Baked Apple Pancake

2 eggs
½ cup all-purpose flour
½ cup milk
¼ cup plus 1 tablespoon butter, divided
6 cups peeled and sliced apples or pears
¼ cup sugar
½ teaspoon ground cinnamon
¼ cup butter, melted

- Preheat oven to 450 degrees.
- Combine eggs, flour, and milk; beat until smooth. Heat an 8-inch ovenproof, non-stick skillet in oven 5 minutes, or until hot. Do not turn off oven. Add 1 tablespoon butter, stirring to coat skillet; pour in batter.
- Bake 10 minutes. Reduce heat to 350 degrees, and bake an additional 10 minutes, or until golden brown.
- Melt remaining ¼ cup butter. Combine apples, sugar, cinnamon, and melted butter in a large saucepan. Cook over medium heat, stirring occasionally, until apples are tender. Spoon mixture onto pancake. Cut into wedges.

Yield: 6 servings

Cheese Strata

8 slices bread, crusts removed
4 processed Cheddar or American cheese slices
Butter
4 eggs, beaten
1⅓ cups milk

- Make 4 sandwiches with the bread and the cheese. Butter both sides of each sandwich heavily. Place in a greased 9 by 13-inch baking dish.
- Combine eggs and the milk, mixing well. Pour over the sandwiches. Let stand overnight in the refrigerator.
- Preheat oven to 350 degrees. Bake for 1 hour, or until set.

Yield: 4 to 6 servings

Variation: Ham slices may also be used for a tasty addition.

Asparagus Cheese Strata

1½ pounds fresh
asparagus, cut into
2-inch pieces
3 tablespoons butter,
melted
1 1-pound loaf sliced
bread, crusts removed
¾ cup shredded Cheddar
cheese, divided
2 cups cubed fully cooked
ham
6 eggs
3 cups milk
2 teaspoons dried minced
onion
½ teaspoon salt
¼ teaspoon dry mustard

• In a saucepan, cover asparagus with water; cover and
cook until just tender. Drain
and set aside.

• Lightly brush the butter over
one side of the bread slices.
Place half of the bread,
buttered side up, in a greased
9 by 13-inch baking dish.
Sprinkle with ½ cup cheese.
Layer with asparagus and
ham. Cover with remaining
bread, buttered side up.

• In a bowl, lightly beat eggs;
add milk, onion, salt and
mustard; pour over bread.
Cover and refrigerate
overnight.

• Preheat oven to 325 degrees.
Bake, uncovered, for
50 minutes. Sprinkle with
remaining cheese. Return to
the oven for 10 minutes or
until cheese is melted and a
knife inserted near the center
comes out clean.

Yield: 10 to 12 servings

Note: Canned asparagus may be substituted.

Asparagus, Ham, and Egg Casserole

8 eggs
3 cups milk
1 tablespoon Dijon
mustard
2 teaspoons dried basil
1 teaspoon salt
2 tablespoons butter,
melted
2 tablespoons flour
2 cups (8 ounces) shredded
Cheddar cheese
1 pound fully cooked ham,
cubed
1 10-ounce package frozen
cut asparagus, thawed,
or 2 cups fresh
asparagus, cooked
2 cups sliced fresh
mushrooms
10 cups cubed bread

- In a large bowl, beat eggs; add milk, mustard, basil, and salt. Gently stir in remaining ingredients until well mixed.
- Pour into a greased 10 by 15-inch baking dish. Cover and refrigerate 8 hours or overnight.
- Remove from the refrigerator 30 minutes before baking. Meanwhile, preheat oven to 350 degrees.
- Bake, uncovered, for 1 hour or until a knife inserted near the center comes out clean. Let stand 5 minutes before cutting.

Yield: 12 servings

Egg and Broccoli Brunch

1 10-ounce package frozen
  chopped broccoli,
  cooked and drained
6 hard-boiled eggs, halved
¼ cup mayonnaise
2 tablespoons Dijon
  mustard
½ cup chopped fully
  cooked ham
1 tablespoon sliced green
  onion

Cheese Sauce

2 tablespoons butter
2 tablespoons flour
1¼ cups milk
Dash of salt
Dash of paprika
1 cup shredded Cheddar
  cheese
2 tablespoons grated
  Parmesan cheese

- Preheat oven to 400 degrees.
- In a greased 7 by 11-inch baking dish, layer broccoli and eggs. Combine the mayonnaise, mustard, ham, and onion; spread over eggs.
- Prepare the Cheese Sauce by melting butter in a saucepan; add flour. Cook and stir until bubbly. Gradually add milk, salt, and paprika; cook and stir until boiling. Cook and stir 2 minutes more. Remove from the heat; stir in Cheddar cheese until melted. Pour over casserole.
- Sprinkle with Parmesan cheese. Bake, uncovered, for 10 to 12 minutes or until heated through.

Yield: 6 servings

Dried Beef and Egg Brunch

4 slices bacon
½ cup (1 stick) butter, divided
½ cup flour
1 quart milk
Pepper
½ pound dried beef, cut coarsely
2 3-ounce cans sliced mushrooms
16 eggs, beaten
¼ teaspoon salt
1 cup evaporated milk

- Preheat oven to 275 degrees.
- Fry bacon in a large skillet until crisp. Remove, drain, and crumble coarsely. Discard bacon grease.
- In same skillet, melt ¼ cup of the butter. Add flour to make a paste. Slowly add milk, stirring constantly to make sauce, adding pepper to taste. Remove from heat; add beef, mushrooms, and crumbled bacon. Set aside.
- In a mixing bowl, mix eggs with salt and evaporated milk; pour remaining ¼ cup butter in a skillet with the beaten eggs and scramble until done but still moist.
- Place a small amount of sauce in the bottom of a greased 3-quart baking dish; layer eggs on top and cover with remaining sauce. (May be prepared to this point one day ahead of time and baked just before serving.)
- Bake covered for 1½ hours.

Yield: 10 to 12 servings

Baked Eggs in Cheese Sauce

3 tablespoons butter
3 tablespoons flour
1½ cups milk
1 teaspoon prepared mustard
½ pound Cheddar cheese, grated
6 eggs
Salt
Pepper

- Preheat oven to 325 degrees.
- Melt butter in a saucepan over low heat; add flour. Gradually add milk, stirring constantly, until smooth. Simmer over medium heat until thickened. Add mustard and cheese and stir until cheese has melted.
- Pour half of cheese sauce into a greased 9 by 9-inch baking dish. Break in eggs; cover with remaining sauce.
- Bake for 20 to 25 minutes.

Yield: 6 servings

Note: Great served with sausage and hot biscuits.

Salsa Eggs

½ cup finely chopped
  sweet red pepper
2 tablespoons butter,
  melted
6 eggs, beaten
1 4-ounce can chopped
  green chiles, drained
1 fresh jalapeño pepper,
  seeded and minced
¼ teaspoon salt
Dash of ground red pepper
Salsa
Sour cream

- Sauté chopped red pepper in butter in a large skillet until tender.
- In a separate bowl, combine eggs, chiles, jalapeño pepper, salt, and red pepper; stir well. Add to skillet.
- Cook over medium-low heat, without stirring, until mixture begins to set on bottom. Draw a spatula across bottom of the skillet to form large curds. Continue cooking until eggs are firm but still moist; do not stir constantly.
- Top each serving with salsa and a dollop of sour cream.

Yield: 3 to 4 servings

French Omelet

3 eggs
3 tablespoons milk
¼ teaspoon salt
⅛ teaspoon pepper
1 tablespoon butter

- Beat eggs slightly; add milk, salt, and pepper, mixing well.

- Melt butter in a skillet over medium heat, rotating pan to coat bottom. Add egg mixture. As it starts to cook, gently lift the edges of the omelet with a spatula, and tilt pan so uncooked portion flows underneath. Continue to cook until top of omelet is set.

- When omelet is set but still shiny, loosen edges with a spatula. If filling is desired, spread over one half of the omelet and gently fold the other side over to cover.

- Invert heated platter over skillet; turn out omelet and serve immediately.

Yield: 2 servings

Spanish-Style Omelets

¼ **cup chopped**
   mushrooms
2 **tablespoons chopped**
   onion
2 **tablespoons chopped**
   celery
2 **tablespoons chopped**
   green pepper
Vegetable oil
1 **8-ounce can tomato**
   sauce
Salt
Dash of hot sauce
6 **eggs**
6 **tablespoons water**

- Sauté vegetables in
  1 tablespoon hot oil until
  tender. Add tomato sauce,
  ¼ teaspoon salt, and hot
  sauce; bring to a boil.
  Set aside.
- Combine 2 of the eggs,
  2 tablespoons water, and a
  pinch of salt; mix just until
  blended.
- Heat a 10-inch omelet pan
  or heavy skillet over medium
  heat until hot enough to
  sizzle a drop of water. Add
  1 tablespoon oil; rotate pan
  to coat bottom. Pour egg
  mixture into skillet. As mixture starts to cook, gently lift
  edges of omelet with a
  spatula, and tilt pan so
  uncooked portion flows
  underneath.
- When egg mixture is set,
  spoon 3 tablespoons sauce
  over half of the omelet.
  Loosen omelet with spatula,
  and fold in half. Gently slide
  omelet onto a serving plate.
- Make 2 additional omelets
  with remaining ingredients.
  Spoon remaining sauce over
  omelets.

Yield: 3 servings

Grits Casserole

½ **cup bell peppers,
chopped**
3 **tablespoons butter**
1 **teaspoon salt**
½ **teaspoon Accent**
Ground red pepper
1 **cup grits**
4 **cups water**
4 **tablespoons pimiento,
chopped**
12 **slices processed
American cheese**

Sauce

3 **tablespoons butter**
3 **tablespoons flour**
1½ **cups milk**
4 **tablespoons onion,
chopped**

- Sauté peppers in butter. Add salt, Accent, red pepper, grits, and water. Slowly bring to a boil; cook until done. Remove from heat.
- Add pimiento and cheese slices. Stir until melted.
- Pour into a 9 by 13-inch baking dish, cover, and refrigerate until cold. Cut into 2-inch squares. Place in a large casserole dish, but do not stir.
- Preheat oven to 350 degrees.
- To make Sauce, melt butter and stir in flour. Gradually add milk, whisking until smooth. Add the onion, stirring constantly until thick.
- Pour the cream sauce over grits squares.
- Bake for 25 to 30 minutes.

Yield: 10 to 12 servings

Quiche

2 ounces butter
½ cup onion, chopped
1 cup diced ham
½ pound Cheddar cheese, grated
1 tablespoon chives
1 tablespoon chopped pimiento
1 9-inch unbaked pie shell
2 extra large eggs (increase number if smaller size used)
¾ cup milk
1 tablespoon flour
Salt
Pepper
Dash of ground red pepper
Dash of nutmeg

- Preheat oven to 400 degrees.
- Melt butter in a small skillet, and sauté onion until golden. Combine onion with ham, cheese, chives, and pimiento, stirring gently. Spoon into pie shell.
- Combine eggs, milk, flour, salt, pepper, red pepper, and nutmeg in a blender. Process until smooth and pour into shell.
- Bake for 20 to 30 minutes, or until knife inserted in the center comes out clean.

Yield: 6 servings

Variation: **Tuna, mushrooms, Monterey Jack cheese**

Salmon, lemon pepper, peas and Monterey Jack cheese

Chicken or turkey with a mild cheese

Ham, asparagus, and Swiss cheese

Crisp cooked bacon and Cheddar cheese

Shrimp, crab, or lobster

Sausage and Cheese Pie

1 9-inch pie crust, baked and slightly cooled
½ pound ground pork sausage
½ pound Cheddar cheese, grated
3 eggs, slightly beaten
½ cup milk
½ teaspoon salt
1 teaspoon lemon juice

- Preheat oven to 325 degrees.
- Sauté sausage in a medium skillet until browned; drain well. Spread sausage over the bottom of the pie shell and top with the Cheddar cheese.
- Combine the eggs, milk, salt, and lemon juice. Mix well and pour into prepared shell.
- Bake for 45 minutes, or until set.

Yield: one 9-inch pie

Crescent Breakfast Brunch

2 8-ounce cans refrigerated crescent dinner rolls
1 pound ground sausage, mild or hot
1 8-ounce package cream cheese, softened

- Preheat oven to 350 degrees.
- Sauté sausage in a skillet until browned; drain well. Combine sausage and cream cheese, mixing well.
- Spread 1 can of the rolls on the bottom of a greased 9 by 13-inch rimmed baking sheet. Seal perforations. Spread sausage mixture evenly on top. Cover with remaining can of rolls, sealing perforations.
- Bake for 15-20 minutes or until browned.

Yield: 15 servings

Variation: Chopped mushrooms and chopped green onions may be added to the sausage-cream cheese mixture.

Breakfast Pizza

1 pound ground pork
   sausage
1 8-ounce can refrigerated
   crescent dinner rolls
1 cup (4 ounces) shredded
   sharp Cheddar cheese
1 cup (4 ounces) shredded
   mozzarella cheese
5 eggs, beaten
¾ teaspoon dried oregano
   leaves
⅛ teaspoon pepper
Green and red pepper
   slices, optional

- Preheat oven to 375 degrees.
- Cook sausage in a medium skillet until browned; drain well. Set aside.
- Separate crescent dough into 8 triangles; place triangles, with elongated points toward center, in a greased 12-inch pizza pan. Press bottom and sides to form a crust. Seal perforations.
- Bake for 5 minutes on lower oven rack. Crust will be puffy when removed from oven. Reduce oven temperature to 350 degrees.
- Spoon sausage over dough; sprinkle with cheeses. Combine eggs, oregano, and pepper; pour over sausage mixture.
- Bake on lower oven rack 30 to 35 minutes. Garnish with green and red pepper slices, if desired.

Yield: 6 to 8 servings

Brunch Tarts

½ **pound ground pork
  sausage**
1¼ **cups biscuit baking
  mix**
¼ **cup butter, softened**
2 **tablespoons boiling
  water**
½ **cup half-and-half**
1 **egg, beaten**
2 **tablespoons thinly-sliced
  green onions**
¼ **teaspoon salt**
½ **cup shredded Swiss
  cheese**

- Preheat oven to 375 degrees. Generously grease 12 large muffin cups or 60 miniature cups.

- Crumble sausage into a skillet and cook until browned, stirring to break up lumps. Drain well.

- Mix baking mix and butter. Add water; stir vigorously until soft dough forms. Press 1 level tablespoon of dough on the bottom and up the side of each cup. Divide sausage evenly among cups.

- Combine half-and-half and egg; stir in onions and salt. Spoon about 1 tablespoon (or 1 teaspoon for miniature) of this mixture into each greased cup. Sprinkle cheese over the top.

- Bake until edges are golden brown and centers are set, about 25 minutes for large tarts or 12 minutes for miniature tarts.

Yield: 12 large tarts or 60 miniature tarts

Frozen Cheese Soufflé

¼ **cup flour**
½ **teaspoon salt**
⅛ **teaspoon red pepper**
3 **tablespoons butter,**
  melted
1 **cup milk**
1½ **cups grated sharp**
  cheese
4 **eggs, separated**
¼ **teaspoon cream of**
  tartar

- In the top of a double boiler over low heat, blend flour, salt, red pepper, and butter. Simmer for a few minutes. Add milk and stir until thickened. Stir in cheese over low heat until melted and mixture is smooth. Remove from heat.

- Beat egg yolks until thick and blend into sauce. Cool.

- Beat egg whites slightly and add cream of tartar. Continue beating until stiff, not dry. Fold cheese mixture into egg whites. Pour into ungreased 1½-quart soufflé or baking dish. Freeze at once.

- To bake, place in a cold oven and turn to 300 degrees. Bake 1½ hours. Serve at once.

Yield: 6 servings

Note: Make ahead of time and freeze until needed.

Oven-Baked French Toast

16 slices white sandwich
   bread, cut into 1-inch
   cubes
1 8-ounce package cream
   cheese, softened
12 large eggs, beaten
2 cups whipping cream
½ cup maple syrup
½ teaspoon maple
   flavoring
Maple syrup

- Place bread cubes in a lightly greased 9 by 13-inch baking dish; set aside.

- Beat cream cheese at medium speed with an electric mixer until smooth; add eggs, whipping cream, syrup, and flavoring, beating until blended. Pour over bread cubes; cover and refrigerate 8 hours or overnight.

- Remove from refrigerator; let stand at room temperature 30 minutes. Meanwhile, preheat oven to 375 degrees.

- Bake for 40 to 50 minutes or until set, covering with foil after 25 minutes. Serve with additional syrup.

Yield: 15 servings

Crispy Waffles

2 cups biscuit mix
½ cup vegetable oil
1 egg, beaten
1⅓ cups club soda

- Mix all ingredients until smooth. Cook in a pre-heated waffle iron for 1½ minutes, or until crisp.

Yield: 3 servings

Waffles

1¾ cups flour
½ teaspoon salt
3 teaspoons baking powder
2 eggs, separated
1¼ cups milk
½ cup shortening, melted

- Preheat waffle iron.
- Sift flour, salt, and baking powder; set aside.
- In a separate bowl, slightly beat egg yolks. Add milk and shortening, mixing well. Stir in sifted dry ingredients.
- In a separate small bowl, beat egg whites until stiffened. Fold into flour mixture.
- Bake in hot iron. Waffles are done when steam no longer appears. Do not raise cover when baking.

Yield: 8 serving

Soups

and

Sandwiches

B. McWilliams

Savory Vegetable Broth

4 beef bouillon cubes
4 cups water
1 stalk celery, sliced
1 large carrot, sliced
1 medium onion, chopped
¼ pound fresh
  mushrooms, chopped
⅓ cup uncooked
  regular rice
⅛ teaspoon pepper

- Soften bouillon cubes in water in a large skillet; Add remaining ingredients, mixing well.
- Bring to a boil; reduce heat, and simmer gently for 30 to 35 minutes or until vegetables are tender, stirring occasionally.

Yield: 1 quart

Cheddar Cheese Soup

2 carrots
1 celery stalk
1 small onion
½ small bell pepper
¼ cup butter
2 garlic cloves, minced
⅓ cup all-purpose flour
1 14½-ounce can chicken
  broth
2 cups milk
4 cups (16 ounces) grated
  Cheddar cheese
½ teaspoon salt
¾ teaspoon pepper
Milk
4 bacon slices, cooked and
  crumbled

- Scrape and thinly slice carrots; finely chop celery, onion, and bell pepper.
- Melt butter in a 3-quart saucepan over medium-high heat; add vegetables and garlic, and cook, stirring constantly, 5 to 7 minutes or until tender.
- Add flour; cook 1 minute, stirring constantly. Stir in broth and 2 cups milk; cook 5 minutes or until mixture is slightly thickened and bubbly.
- Add grated cheese, salt, and pepper, stirring until well-blended. Stir in additional milk, if necessary, to reach desired consistency. Sprinkle soup with crumbled bacon.

Yield: 7 cups

Vegetable Beef Soup

2 pounds beef stew meat
without fat
2 medium to large onions,
chopped
2 medium potatoes,
chopped
3 carrots, sliced (half
slices, if large)
8 to 10 ounces okra,
small pods, fresh or
frozen, sliced
½ cup chopped bell pepper
½ cup kernel corn
¾ cup English peas
¾ cup butterbeans
1 14½-ounce can tomato
wedges
2 cups spicy or regular
tomato juice
1 tablespoon salt
¼ teaspoon freshly ground
black pepper (may use
up to ½ teaspoon)
2 or 3 large bay leaves
2 or 3 tablespoons finely-
snipped parsley (use
scissors to make this
easy)

- Cut stew meat into ½ to
¾-inch cubes. Cook, in water
to cover, overnight in a slow
cooker.

- Add water to make a total of
about 2 quarts. Pour into a
2-gallon stock pot. Stir in
remaining ingredients.
Bring to a boil, stirring
occasionally; simmer several
hours, covered.

- To freeze any remaining
soup, put leftover soup in
containers, freezing all that
will not be eaten within 2 or
3 days.

Yield: approximately 1½ gallons

*Note: Any vegetable can be omitted or used in a greater or
lesser amount.*

Chicken Soup

1 2½ to 3-pound chicken
3 quarts water
1 tablespoon salt
1 medium onion
6 whole peppercorns
6 celery stalks, reserving
   leaves, divided
6 whole medium carrots,
   divided
2 cups cooked rice or
   cooked fine egg noodles
¼ cup chopped fresh
   parsley
3 to 4 drops yellow food
   coloring

• Put chicken, water, salt, onion, peppercorns, 3 of the celery stalks, all the celery leaves, and 3 carrots in stock pot. Cover and bring to boil. Skim off foam. Reduce heat to simmer and cook until meat is very tender, about 2 hours.

• Remove chicken and vegetables. Strain stock. Chill several hours or overnight.

• Dice remaining 3 stalks celery and 3 carrots. Add to stock and cook until tender.

• Meanwhile, bone chicken; dice meat. Add chicken, cooked rice or noodles, and parsley. Heat thoroughly. Stir in food coloring.

Yield: 10 to 12 servings

Creamy Asparagus Soup

½ cup chopped onion
1 cup sliced celery
3 cloves garlic, pressed
3 tablespoons butter,
   melted
2 14½-ounce cans cut
   asparagus, undrained
1 16-ounce can sliced
   potatoes, drained or
   2 cooked, peeled, and
   sliced potatoes
1 14½-ounce can chicken
   broth
1 teaspoon white vinegar
1 teaspoon salt
½ teaspoon ground black
   pepper
¼ teaspoon ground red
   pepper
½ teaspoon dried basil
1 cup milk
½ cup sour cream, optional
Celery leaves for garnish,
   optional

- Cook onion, celery, and garlic in butter in a Dutch oven over medium-high heat, stirring constantly, until tender. Stir in asparagus, potatoes, chicken broth, vinegar, salt, black pepper, red pepper, and basil.

- Bring to a boil, stirring often. Reduce heat, and simmer, uncovered, 10 minutes, stirring often. Cool slightly.

- Pour half of mixture into container of an electric blender; process until smooth, stopping once to scrape down sides. Transfer mixture to separate bowl. Repeat procedure with other half of mixture.

- Return asparagus mixture to Dutch oven. Stir in milk; cook just until thoroughly heated (do not boil). Dollop each serving with sour cream; garnish, if desired.

Yield: 2 quarts

Note: May prepare vegetable puree base ahead of time; refrigerate up to three days or freeze up to six months. Dilute with milk, and heat to serve.

Broccoli Cheese Soup

2 14½-ounce cans chicken
  broth or 3½ cups
  homemade broth
2 pounds fresh broccoli,
  chopped
3 cups milk
1 cup diced cooked ham
1 teaspoon salt
Pinch of onion salt
¼ teaspoon black pepper
¼ teaspoon dried thyme
1 cup half-and-half
½ pound grated Cheddar
  cheese
4 tablespoons butter,
  softened

- Combine broth and broccoli in a large saucepan. Bring to a boil; cook 7 minutes. Strain broth into another pan. Puree broccoli in a food processor.
- To the broth, add pureed broccoli, milk, ham, salt, and pepper. Bring to a boil, turn down heat, and simmer 5 minutes.
- Stir in remaining ingredients, cooking until heated through.

Yield: 8 servings

Sausage and Bean Soup

1 pound ground pork
  sausage
2 16-ounce cans kidney
  beans, drained
1 28-ounce can tomatoes,
  chopped
4 cups water
1 large onion, chopped
1 bay leaf
½ teaspoon salt
½ teaspoon garlic salt
½ teaspoon thyme
⅛ teaspoon pepper
½ cup chopped bell
  pepper

- Cook sausage until browned. Drain and crumble.
- In a large pot, combine beans, tomatoes, water, onion, bay leaf, salt, garlic salt, thyme, and pepper. Add sausage; cover and simmer 1 hour.
- Stir in bell pepper; cook 15 to 20 minutes, or until bell pepper is tender.

Yield: 6 servings

Eastern Suburbia Soup

1 small head cabbage or
   1 small bag commercially-
   prepared coleslaw mix
1 onion
1 bunch parsley
3 14½-ounce cans chicken
   broth, divided (can use
   more if needed)
6 10¾-ounce cans potato
   soup
1 lemon, juiced
1 cup cooked chopped ham
4 cups sour cream (may use
   low-fat or no-fat)
Sherry, optional

- Cut cabbage and onion into chunks; mince in food processor with parsley. If using coleslaw mix, process onion with parsley and add to cabbage.
- In a covered stock pot or Dutch oven, cook cabbage mixture in 1 cup of the broth until tender.
- Stir in the remaining ingredients and remaining broth; simmer for 1 hour.

Yield: 16 servings

Corn Chowder

6 slices bacon
1 medium onion, coarsely
   chopped
2 medium potatoes, peeled
   and cubed
½ cup water
2 cups milk
1 15-ounce can cream-
   style corn
½ teaspoon salt
Dash of black pepper

- Fry bacon in a Dutch oven until crisp. Remove and drain, reserving 2 tablespoons drippings. Crumble bacon; set aside.
- Sauté onion in drippings until tender. Add potatoes and water. Cover and simmer 15 to 20 minutes, or until tender.
- Stir in remaining ingredients. Cook over medium heat, stirring frequently, until heated. Sprinkle each serving with crumbled bacon.

Yield: 5 cups

71

Baked Potato Soup

**4 large white or baking
potatoes**
⅔ cup butter
⅔ cup all-purpose flour
6 cups milk
¾ teaspoon salt
½ teaspoon pepper
**4 green onions, chopped,
divided**
**12 slices bacon, cooked
and crumbled, divided**
**1¼ cups (5 ounces) grated
Cheddar cheese, divided**
**1 8-ounce carton sour
cream**

- Wash potatoes; bake at
  400 degrees 1 hour. Scoop
  out pulp.
- In a stock pot or Dutch oven,
  melt butter; add flour. Cook
  on low 1 minute. Add milk;
  cook over medium heat until
  thickened, stirring constantly.
- Add potato pulp, salt,
  pepper, 2 tablespoons of
  the green onion, ½ of the
  bacon, and 1 cup of the
  cheese. Cook until heated
  thoroughly.
- Stir in sour cream. Add extra
  milk, if necessary, for desired
  thickness.
- Serve with remaining onion,
  bacon, and cheese on top.

Yield: 12 servings

*Note: Top leftover potato skins with additional crisp bacon,
chopped green onion, grated cheese, salt, and pepper; broil until
cheese is melted. Add a dollop of sour cream and serve with soup.*

Gazpacho

6 medium tomatoes,
  peeled and chopped
  (3 cups)
1 cup chopped bell pepper
1 cup peeled, seeded, and
  chopped cucumber
½ cup canned sliced or
  chopped beets
½ cup chopped celery
¼ cup chopped onion
2 cloves garlic, minced
1 cup beef consommé,
  undiluted
¼ cup red wine vinegar
¼ cup olive oil
2 tablespoons paprika
2 teaspoons salt
1 teaspoon dried basil
¼ teaspoon hot sauce
Cucumber slices, optional
Sour cream, optional

- Place half of tomatoes in container of an electric blender; process until smooth, stopping once to scrape down sides.
- Gradually add half each of bell pepper, cucumber, beets, celery, onion, and garlic; process until smooth. Add half each of consommé, wine vinegar, olive oil, paprika, salt, basil, and hot sauce; process until smooth. Transfer to a bowl.
- Repeat procedure with remaining ingredients. Cover and chill 8 hours.
- Garnish with cucumber slices and a dollop of sour cream, if desired.

Yield: 9 cups

Zesty Steak Chili

**4 pounds round steak, cut
into 1-inch cubes**
4 cloves garlic, minced
¼ cup vegetable oil
3 cups chopped onion
2¾ cups water, divided
2 cups sliced celery
**3 14½-ounce cans diced
tomatoes, undrained**
**2 15-ounce cans tomato
sauce**
1 16-ounce jar salsa
3 tablespoons chili powder
2 teaspoons ground cumin
2 teaspoons dried oregano
1 teaspoon salt, optional
1 teaspoon pepper
¼ cup all-purpose flour
¼ cup yellow cornmeal
**Grated Cheddar cheese,
sour cream, sliced green
onions and sliced ripe
olives, optional**

- In a Dutch oven over medium-high heat, sauté steak
and garlic in oil until
browned. Add onion;
cook and stir 5 minutes.

- Stir in 2 cups of the water,
the celery, tomatoes, tomato
sauce, salsa, chili powder,
cumin, oregano, salt, and
pepper; bring to a boil.
Reduce heat; cover and
simmer 2 hours or until
tender.

- Combine flour, cornmeal,
and the remaining ¾ cup of
water; stir until smooth.
Bring chili to a boil. Add flour
mixture; cook and stir
2 minutes or until thickened.
Garnish with cheese, sour
cream, onions, and olives.

Yield: 20 servings

Cream of Oyster and Spinach Soup

1½ quarts oysters
3 cups water
2 pounds frozen chopped
spinach
6 tablespoons butter
⅔ cup chopped onion
2 stalks celery, chopped
6 tablespoons all-purpose
flour
1 quart milk
½ teaspoon garlic salt or
fresh minced garlic
Pinch of nutmeg
2 tablespoons steak sauce
Salt
Pepper
1 quart half-and-half,
whipped

- Cook oysters in water until done or firm; drain, reserving liquid and keeping hot. Puree oysters in food processor. Refrigerate until ready to use.

- Cook spinach according to package directions; drain well. Puree in processor. Set aside.

- Melt butter in Dutch oven over medium heat; add onion and celery. Sauté, stirring constantly, until clear. Push onions and celery to side of pan; sprinkle flour over butter. Stir to make a paste. Slowly add milk, stirring constantly. Pour in the hot reserved oyster liquid, whisking to make smooth. Simmer, uncovered, 30 minutes.

- Add pureed oysters and spinach. Stir in garlic salt or fresh garlic, nutmeg, steak sauce, and salt and pepper to taste.

- Add cream before serving, heating thoroughly but not allowing to boil.

Yield: 18 to 20 servings

Oyster Artichoke Soup

½ cup chopped green
onions

½ pound fresh mushrooms,
rinsed and sliced

¼ pound (1 stick) butter,
melted

¼ teaspoon ground red
pepper

4 tablespoons all-purpose
flour

1 14½-ounce can chicken
broth

1 pint oysters, drained,
reserving liquid (may cut
oysters in half, if large)

1 14-ounce can artichoke
hearts, finely chopped

¼ teaspoon Tabasco

2 cups milk, heated

1 tablespoon chopped
parsley

- Sauté onion and mushrooms in butter in a large saucepan. Season with pepper. Add flour and whisk well. Stir in chicken broth and oyster liquid until smooth.

- Mix in artichokes, Tabasco, and milk. Gently stir in oysters and parsley. Simmer 15 minutes, or until oysters begin to curl.

Yield: 4 to 6 servings

Crab and Asparagus Soup

¼ cup chopped green
   onions
1 tablespoon butter
½ teaspoon curry powder
2 10¾-ounce cans cream
   of asparagus soup
2 7½-ounce cans crabmeat
1 pint half-and-half
¼ cup sherry

- In a large saucepan or Dutch oven, sauté onion in butter. Stir in curry powder, mixing well.

- Add soup, crabmeat, and half-and-half; simmer until heated, but do not boil.

- Pour in sherry; simmer 5 additional minutes.

Yield: 8 servings

Variation: To give color, add 1 10-ounce can drained and mashed asparagus.

Crab Bisque

3 green onions, chopped
1 pound plus 4
   tablespoons (2½ sticks)
   butter, melted
1 to 2 pounds crabmeat
2 14½-ounce cans chicken
   broth
2 pints whipping cream
4 heaping tablespoons
   cornstarch
Salt

- In a stock pot or Dutch oven, sauté onion in butter until tender. Remove from heat. Stir in crabmeat; allow to stand 5 minutes to soak in butter.

- Return to heat. Stir in chicken broth; bring to a boil. Reduce heat to medium; add whipping cream.

- Combine cornstarch and small amount of water to make a smooth paste. Add slowly to crabmeat mixture, stirring constantly, until thickened. Season with salt to taste.

- Simmer for a few minutes, allowing flavors to blend.

Yield: 15 servings

77

Shrimp Bisque

1 pound unpeeled,
   medium-size fresh
   shrimp
4 tablespoons butter
1 cup sliced fresh
   mushrooms
¼ cup chopped green
   onions
1 clove garlic, minced
3 tablespoons all-purpose
   flour
1 10½-ounce can
   condensed chicken
   broth, undiluted
½ cup dry white wine
½ cup whipping cream
1 tablespoon chopped
   fresh parsley

- Peel shrimp, and devein, if desired; set shrimp aside.
- Melt butter in a large heavy saucepan. Add mushrooms, green onions, and garlic; sauté 5 minutes or until vegetables are tender.
- Add flour to sauce, stirring until mixture is smooth; cook over medium heat, stirring constantly, 1 minute. Gradually add chicken broth to pan; cook, stirring constantly, until mixture is thickened and bubbly.
- Add shrimp; reduce heat, and simmer 3 minutes, stirring often. Stir in wine, whipping cream, and parsley; cook until thoroughly heated, stirring often.

Yield: 1 quart

Seafood Gumbo

4 tablespoons oil
⅔ cup all-purpose flour
2 large onions, chopped
2 cloves garlic, minced
1½ cups chopped ham
6 cups chopped okra
4 quarts water
3 tablespoons
  Worcestershire sauce
3 16-ounce cans tomatoes
Dash of Tabasco
Salt
Pepper
2 to 4 pounds raw shrimp,
  peeled and deveined
1 pound crabmeat
4 to 5 bay leaves, optional
Hot cooked rice

• Heat oil in a heavy skillet. Stir in flour; brown slowly until a very dark caramel color. Add onion and garlic; brown. Mix in ham; brown. Add okra; continue to brown mixture very slowly for 1 hour or more.

• In a large pot, bring water, Worcestershire sauce, tomatoes, Tabasco, salt and pepper to a boil. Add browned mixture; cook slowly 4 hours.

• Gently stir in shrimp and crabmeat; simmer 2 hours.

• Add bay leaves 1 hour before serving, if desired. Serve over rice in a large bowl.

Yield: 6 to 8 servings

Note: May be prepared several days ahead. Freezes well.

79

French Dip Sandwich

1 3½-to-4 pound boneless
chuck roast, trimmed
½ cup soy sauce
1 beef bouillon cube
1 bay leaf
3 to 4 peppercorns
1 teaspoon dried
rosemary, crushed
1 teaspoon dried thyme
1 teaspoon garlic powder
12 French sandwich rolls,
split

• Place roast in a 5-quart slow
cooker. Combine soy sauce,
bouillon cube, bay leaf,
peppercorns, rosemary,
thyme, and garlic powder;
pour over roast. Add water
until roast is almost covered.

• Cook, covered, on low
7 hours, or until very tender.
Remove roast, reserving
broth; shred roast with a
fork. Place roast in rolls;
serve with reserved broth
for dipping.

Yield: 12 servings

Grilled Sour Cream Burgers

½ cup commercial sour
cream-French onion dip,
plus extra for buns
3 tablespoons fine dry
bread crumbs
¼ teaspoon salt
Dash of pepper
1 pound ground beef
4 hamburger buns,
buttered and toasted

• Combine dip, bread crumbs,
salt, and pepper in a bowl;
mix well. Add ground beef;
stir until blended. Shape into
4 patties about ½-inch thick.

• Grill over medium coals
6 to 8 minutes on each side.
Serve on buns with additional
sour cream dip, if desired.

Yield: 4 servings

Hot Ham and Cheese Sandwiches

2 cups butter, melted
3 tablespoons minced
onion
3 tablespoons prepared
mustard
3 tablespoons horseradish
3 tablespoons poppy seeds
30 commercially-prepared
buns
4 pounds paper-thin sliced
ham
30 slices Swiss cheese
30 slices American cheese

- Combine butter, onion, mustard, horseradish, and poppy seeds in a bowl.
- Spread butter mixture on both sides of bun. Layer ham on bottom half of bun; add a layer of both cheeses. Cover with bun tops. Drizzle any remaining butter mixture on top of bun.
- Wrap each sandwich well in foil; freeze. When ready to serve, bake frozen sandwiches in a 350 degree oven 30 minutes.

Yield: 30 servings

Carrot Salad Sandwich

½ cup raisins
1 8-ounce can crushed
pineapple, drained,
reserving juice
1 pound carrots,
processed until finely
minced
2 tablespoons mayonnaise
24 slices thin bread or
36 party-size slices,
crusts trimmed

- Place raisins in reserved pineapple juice; let sit until raisins are plump. Drain raisins; combine with pineapple, processed carrot, and mayonnaise. (Add more mayonnaise to taste, if necessary.)
- Spread carrot mixture on bread slices.

Yield: 12 whole sandwiches or 36 open-faced party sandwiches

81

Hot Pepperoni Bread

1 loaf frozen bread dough
12 ounces pepperoni,
  sliced
1 6-ounce package
  mozzarella cheese, sliced
1 6-ounce package
  provolone cheese, sliced
2 eggs, beaten
Parmesan and/or Romano
  cheese, grated

- Thaw bread dough; let rise in a large oiled bowl. Cover and let sit for 4 to 5 hours, or until doubled in bulk.

- Roll dough out in a ⅛-to-¼-inch thick rectangle on a floured board (the thinner the better). Top with pepperoni slices, mozzarella slices, and provolone slices. Pieces should touch or lap, but not be stacked. Brush with half of the beaten egg. Sprinkle with grated cheeses.

- Roll jelly roll-fashion; place seam side down on greased baking sheet, either straight, in a circle, or horseshoe shape. Pinch ends shut. Brush with remaining beaten egg on sides and top. Place greased waxed paper and two dish towels on loaf; let rise 30 to 40 minutes.

- Preheat oven to 400 degrees.

- Bake 20 minutes; reduce heat to 350 degrees and continue baking 10 minutes, or until dark brown. Cool slightly; slice.

Yield: 8 servings

Note: *May be used as an appetizer or as a main dish with a green salad.*

Variation: *Substitute cooked sausage or baked ham for pepperoni.*

Hot Crab and Cheese Sandwich

½ cup chopped green
  onions
½ cup chopped sweet red
  pepper
1 tablespoon butter,
  melted
½ pound fresh crabmeat,
  drained and flaked
1 cup (4 ounces) grated
  Cheddar cheese
1 cup (4 ounces) grated
  Monterey Jack cheese
⅓ cup cream of celery
  soup, undiluted
3 English muffins, split and
  toasted

- Preheat oven to 350 degrees.
- Cook green onions and pepper in butter in a skillet over medium-high heat, stirring constantly, until tender. Remove from heat; stir in crabmeat, Cheddar cheese, Monterey Jack cheese, and soup.
- Mound mixture in centers of muffin halves. (Do not spread to edges.) Place muffin halves on a lightly greased baking sheet.
- Bake 15 minutes, or until thoroughly heated.

Yield: 3 to 6 servings

Basic Pimiento Cheese

12 ounces medium
  Cheddar cheese, grated
8 ounces sharp Cheddar
  cheese, grated
1 4-ounce jar pimiento,
  drained and diced
1 cup mayonnaise
2 teaspoons grated onion,
  optional

- Combine all ingredients, mixing well.
- Refrigerate for a few hours, allowing flavors to blend.

Yield: 6 cups

83

Spinach Sandwich

**1 10-ounce box frozen
chopped spinach, thawed
and squeezed dry**
**½ cup finely chopped
water chestnuts**
1 tablespoon mayonnaise
2 tablespoons sour cream
**3 green onions, finely
chopped**
1 teaspoon salt
**¼ teaspoon ground black
pepper**
½ lemon, juiced
¼ teaspoon Accent
**½ teaspoon Worcestershire
sauce**
**24 slices bread or
36 party-size slices,
crusts trimmed**

- Combine all ingredients.
  Add more mayonnaise,
  if needed.
- Spread bread slices with
  spinach mixture.

Yield: 12 whole sandwiches or 36 open-faced party sandwiches

Note: Good on white, rye, or wheat bread

Salads

and

Dressings

Waldorf Salad

2 tablespoons orange juice
3 large tart red apples,
  peeled, cored, and diced
½ cup diced celery
½ cup sour cream
½ cup raisins
¼ cup chopped walnuts or
  pecans
1½ teaspoons sugar

- Sprinkle orange juice over apples; toss and drain.
- Add remaining ingredients. Stir well. Cover and chill.

Yield: 6 servings

Lemon-Lime Salad

1 3-ounce package lemon
  Jell-o
1 3-ounce package lime
  Jell-o
2 cups boiling water
1 cup mayonnaise
1 14-ounce can sweetened
  condensed milk
1 cup small curd cottage
  cheese
1 cup crushed pineapple,
  drained
1 cup chopped nuts

- Combine Jell-o with water, stirring to dissolve. Cool slightly.
- Stir in remaining ingredients; mix well.
- Congeal until set in a greased 9-cup mold.

Yield: 8 to 10 servings

Orange Fluff Salad

2 3-ounce packages orange Jell-o
2 cups boiling water
1 6-ounce can frozen orange juice concentrate, undiluted
1 20-ounce can crushed pineapple, drained
2 15-ounce cans Mandarin oranges, drained

Topping

1 3.4-ounce package lemon instant pudding
1 cup cold milk
1 6-ounce carton frozen whipped topping

- Mix Jell-o and water in a greased 9 by 13-inch dish, stirring until dissolved. Stir in orange juice concentrate until combined. Add pineapple and oranges; refrigerate until congealed.
- To make Topping, combine pudding and milk; fold in whipped topping. Spread on top of salad. Cut into squares and serve.

Yield: 12 servings

Frozen Fruit Salad

1 8-ounce carton frozen whipped topping
1 8-ounce carton sour cream
1 6-ounce bottle maraschino cherries, drained and chopped
1 15-ounce can crushed pineapple, drained
5 bananas, peeled and mashed
1 cup chopped pecans

- Combine all ingredients; mix well and spoon into an 8-inch square pan.
- Cover with foil and freeze. Remove from freezer 30 minutes before serving.
- To serve, cut into squares.

Yield: 8 to 10 servings

Raspberry Congealed Salad

1 8-ounce can crushed pineapple
1 10-ounce package frozen unsweetened raspberries, thawed
1 3-ounce package raspberry Jell-o
1 cup applesauce
¼ cup coarsely chopped pecans
Mayonnaise, optional

- Drain pineapple and raspberries, reserving juices. Place fruit in a large bowl; set aside.
- Add enough water to the juice to measure 1 cup. Pour into a saucepan; bring to a boil. Remove from the heat; stir in Jell-o until dissolved. Pour over fruit mixture. Add the applesauce and pecans. Pour into a 1-quart bowl or mold. Chill until set.
- Spoon into individual dessert dishes; top with a dollop of mayonnaise, if desired.

Yield: 6 servings

Congealed Shrimp Salad

1 10¾-ounce can tomato soup
1 8-ounce package cream cheese
2 envelopes unflavored gelatin
¾ cup cold water
1 cup mayonnaise
½ cup chopped onions
½ cup chopped celery
½ cup chopped olives
3 hard-boiled eggs, chopped
2 6-ounce cans shrimp

- In a saucepan, combine the soup and cream cheese until cheese dissolves.
- In a small mixing bowl, mix the gelatin and water. Add to soup mixture and beat until creamy.
- Fold in remaining ingredients; pour into a greased dish and congeal.

Yield: 8 servings

Congealed Tuna Salad

4 6-ounce cans albacore
  tuna
2 lemons, juiced
1 cup chopped olives
4 hard-boiled eggs,
  chopped
3 tablespoons chopped
  green onions
1 cup chopped celery
2 envelopes unflavored
  gelatin
⅔ cup cold water
2 cups mayonnaise plus
  extra for garnish
Lettuce leaves
Paprika

- Combine tuna, lemon juice, olives, eggs, green onions, and celery. Set aside.
- Soak gelatin in water for 5 minutes. Dissolve over hot water or in microwave. Add mayonnaise. Fold into tuna mixture.
- Pour into a 9 by 13-inch dish; congeal. Cut into squares. Serve on lettuce leaves with a dash of mayonnaise and paprika.

Yield: 12 to 15 servings

Frozen Strawberry Salad

1 8-ounce package cream
  cheese, softened
1 10-ounce package frozen
  strawberries, chopped
1 15½-ounce can crushed
  pineapple, drained
1 8-ounce carton frozen
  whipped topping, thawed
2 bananas, diced, optional
1 cup chopped nuts,
  optional

- Combine all ingredients. Pour into a 9 by 13-inch dish; freeze.

Yield: 24 servings

Note: Easy to make ahead and keep in freezer.

Cranberry Freeze

3 cups fresh cranberries, finely chopped
1½ cups sugar
1 8-ounce package cream cheese, softened
1 8-ounce can crushed pineapple, drained
½ cup chopped walnuts
1 cup whipping cream, whipped

- Combine cranberries and sugar, stirring well. Allow to stand for 10 minutes or until sugar dissolves, stirring frequently.
- In a separate bowl, beat cream cheese; add pineapple, stirring well. Stir in walnuts and cranberry mixture. Fold in whipped cream.
- Spoon mixture into a lightly greased 7½-cup mold or fill 14 paper-lined muffin pans. Freeze.

Yield: 14 servings

Note: If gelatin mold is used, move salad from freezer to refrigerator 30 minutes before serving. Good to keep in freezer and use when needed.

Cranberry Salad

2 oranges, seeded and
quartered, reserving
juice
1 16-ounce package
cranberries
2 cups sugar
¼ teaspoon salt
1 3-ounce package
raspberry Jell-o
½ 3-ounce package orange
Jell-o

- Process oranges in a food processor until minced. Pour any resulting juice into a 2-cup measuring cup. Place processed orange in a mixing bowl.

- Process cranberries in processor, pouring any juice into measuring cup with orange juice. Add cranberries to oranges in mixing bowl. Stir in sugar and salt. Set aside.

- Add enough water to the orange-cranberry juice to make 2 cups. Heat to boiling in a small saucepan or in the microwave. Mix in raspberry and orange Jell-o, stirring to dissolve.

- Pour Jell-o into cranberry mixture. Pour into a 9 by 13-inch dish. Chill until firm.

Yield: 12 servings

Tomato Aspic

6 cups tomato juice
½ teaspoon salt
1 tablespoon confectioners' sugar
1 teaspoon Worcestershire sauce
Dash of red pepper
Dash of celery salt
2 bay leaves
Celery leaves
1 small onion, chopped
4 envelopes unflavored gelatin
1 cup cold water
2 to 3 tablespoons lemon juice
1 cup finely chopped celery
1 cup chopped olives

Dressing

2 cups sour cream
1 cup mayonnaise
Worcestershire sauce
Parsley flakes
Dash of salt

- In a saucepan, combine the tomato juice, salt, sugar, Worcestershire sauce, pepper, celery salt, bay leaves, celery leaves, and onion. Simmer 20 minutes.
- Meanwhile, soak gelatin in water.
- Strain juice; add gelatin and lemon juice. Chill until consistency of egg white. Add celery and olives. Pour into a 9 by 13-inch baking dish or 12 individual molds. Continue to chill until set.
- To make Dressing, combine sour cream, mayonnaise, Worcestershire sauce, parsley flakes, and salt to taste. Serve over salad.

Yield: 12 servings

Seafood Tomato Aspic

4 cups tomato juice, spicy vegetable juice, or clam-tomato juice
3 tablespoons lemon juice
1/3 cup green onions, finely chopped
1 cup celery, minced
2 cloves garlic, crushed
3 tablespoons Worcestershire sauce
1/4 cup green or red bell pepper, finely chopped
1 14-ounce can artichoke hearts, drained and finely chopped
4 envelopes gelatin, divided
1 6-ounce can shrimp, drained and deveined
1 8-ounce package cream cheese, softened
1/4 cup mayonnaise
1/2 cup pecans, finely chopped
1 4 1/2-ounce can lump crabmeat, drained

• Mix tomato juice, lemon juice, green onion, celery, garlic, Worcestershire sauce, bell pepper, and artichoke hearts in a large mixing bowl. Set aside.

• Place 4 envelopes gelatin in 1 cup cold water for 5 minutes. Heat in microwave for 30 to 45 seconds, just until gelatin is dissolved. Mix 3/4 cup gelatin in tomato juice mixture; reserve 1/4 cup gelatin for later use. Stir in shrimp. Fill one large mold or two smaller molds 1/3 full with this mixture; congeal.

• Mix cream cheese, mayonnaise, pecans, crabmeat, a little more celery and onions to taste, and a dash of Worcestershire sauce and lemon juice. Add remaining 1/4 cup gelatin. Spread cream cheese mixture over tomato juice layer; congeal.

• Pour in another layer of tomato mixture; congeal.

• To serve, unmold onto a lettuce lined tray.

Yield: 12 servings

Note: If served during Christmas, may add a dash or two of green food coloring in the cream cheese layer.

Greek Salad

½ head green leaf lettuce
½ head iceberg lettuce
2 tomatoes, cut in wedges
1 purple onion, sliced
Greek olives

Dressing

6 tablespoons wine vinegar
⅔ cup olive oil
Pinch of salt
Pinch of ground mustard
Feta cheese

- Make salad by combining leaf lettuce, iceberg lettuce, tomatoes, purple onion, and olives.
- To make Dressing, mix the vinegar, olive oil, salt, and mustard.
- Pour Dressing over salad and toss, coating lettuce well. Crumble cheese over dressing to taste.

Yield: 10 servings

Raspberry-Walnut Salad

4 cups torn Boston lettuce
4 cups torn red leaf lettuce
¾ cup chopped walnuts, toasted
1 cup fresh raspberries
1 avocado, peeled and cubed
1 kiwifruit, peeled and sliced

Raspberry Salad Dressing

⅓ cup seedless raspberry jam
⅓ cup raspberry vinegar
1 cup vegetable oil
1 tablespoon poppy seeds

- Combine the Boston lettuce, leaf lettuce, walnuts, raspberries, avocado, and kiwifruit in a large bowl; toss gently.
- For the Dressing, combine the jam and vinegar in container of an electric blender; process 20 seconds. With blender on high, gradually add oil in a slow, steady stream. Stir in poppy seeds. Toss with lettuce and serve.

Yield: 12 servings

Spinach Salad

1 pound fresh spinach
1 cup strawberries, halved
1 cup pecan halves,
   toasted

Poppy Seed Dressing

⅓ cup cider vinegar
⅓ cup vegetable oil
¼ cup sugar
1 tablespoon Dijon
   mustard
1 teaspoon salt
½ teaspoon pepper
1 small onion, chopped
2 teaspoons poppy seeds

• Remove stems from spinach, wash leaves thoroughly, and pat dry. Tear into bite-size pieces. Combine spinach, strawberries, and pecans.

• To make the Dressing, combine the vinegar, vegetable oil, sugar, mustard, salt, pepper, and onion in container of an electric blender; process until smooth. Stir in poppy seeds. Drizzle over spinach. Serve immediately.

Yield: 6 servings

Crunchy Romaine Toss

1 cup walnuts, chopped
1 3-ounce package
  uncooked ramen
  noodles, broken up
  (discard flavor packet)
4 tablespoons unsalted
  butter
1 bunch broccoli, coarsely
  chopped
1 head romaine lettuce,
  washed and torn into
  bite-size pieces
4 green onions, chopped

- In a small skillet, brown walnuts and noodles in butter; cool on paper towels. Toss with broccoli, lettuce, and onions, mixing well.
- To make Dressing, combine all ingredients in a jar; shake vigorously to blend. Pour over vegetable mixture and toss to coat evenly.

Sweet and Sour Dressing

1 cup vegetable oil
1 cup sugar
½ cup wine vinegar
3 teaspoons soy sauce
Salt
Pepper

Yield: 10 to 12 servings

Cabbage Crunch

1 large cabbage, shredded
1 bunch green onions,
chopped
1 2-ounce package sliced
almonds
¼ cup sesame seeds
1 tablespoon butter
2 3-ounce packages ramen
noodles, crushed

- Combine cabbage and green onions. Sauté almonds and sesame seeds in butter until lightly browned. Stir almonds, sesame seeds, and ramen noodles into cabbage and green onions.
- To make Dressing, combine all ingredients in a jar or bowl, mixing well. Pour over cabbage just before serving.

Dressing

¾ cup vegetable oil
6 tablespoons vinegar
4 tablespoons sugar
1 tablespoon Accent
1 teaspoon salt
1 teaspoon pepper

Yield: 12 servings

Note: Goes well with anything on the grill.

Asparagus Vinaigrette

**1½ cups olive or
vegetable oil
½ cup white wine vinegar
2 teaspoons Dijon mustard
½ teaspoon salt
⅛ teaspoon pepper
3 to 4 radishes, sliced
¼ cup chopped bell pepper
3 tablespoons dill pickle
relish
1 tablespoon chopped
fresh parsley
1 tablespoon snipped fresh
chives
2 pounds fresh asparagus
spears, cooked and
drained
Lettuce leaves
3 hard-boiled eggs, sliced
2 medium tomatoes, cut
into wedges**

- In a bowl, whisk together the oil, vinegar, mustard, salt, and pepper. Add radishes, bell pepper, relish, parsley, and chives. Place asparagus in a glass baking dish; pour dressing over asparagus. Cover and chill at least 4 hours or overnight.

- To serve, arrange lettuce on a serving platter; remove asparagus from dressing with a slotted spoon and arrange over lettuce. Garnish with eggs and tomatoes. Drizzle with some of the dressing.

Yield: 6 to 8 servings

Broccoli Salad

7 cups fresh broccoli,
chopped fine
3 cups fresh cauliflower,
chopped fine
1 cup pecans, chopped and
toasted
½ purple onion, chopped
fine
½ pound bacon, cooked
and crumbled
⅓ cup raisins
1 11-ounce can Mandarin
oranges, drained
1 8-ounce can sliced water
chestnuts, drained

Dressing

2 tablespoons vinegar
½ cup sugar
1 cup mayonnaise

- In a large bowl, combine broccoli, cauliflower, pecans, onion, bacon, raisins, oranges, and water chestnuts, mixing well.
- To prepare Dressing, heat vinegar in a small bowl in the microwave; add sugar, stirring to dissolve. Cool slightly, and stir in mayonnaise.
- Pour Dressing over vegetable mixture. Stir lightly to blend.

Yield: 15 servings

Deviled Eggs

12 hard boiled eggs
¼ cup mayonnaise
3 tablespoons
  commercially-
  prepared Thousand
  Island dressing
1½ tablespoons sweet
  pickle relish
¼ teaspoon dry mustard
⅛ teaspoon salt
3 slices bacon, cooked and
  crumbled
Pickle slices
Paprika

- Peel eggs: slice in half length-wise, and carefully remove yolks. Mash yolks; add mayonnaise, and stir well. Stir in salad dressing, relish, mustard, and salt. Stir in crumbled bacon.
- Spoon yolk mixture into egg whites. Garnish halves with pickle slices and sprinkle of paprika.

Yield: 12 servings

Marinated Okra

½ cup vegetable oil
3 tablespoons vinegar
½ teaspoon salt
¼ teaspoon pepper
½ teaspoon Tabasco
1 pound whole okra pods
1 small onion, sliced into
  rings
1 clove garlic

- In a small bowl, combine oil, vinegar, salt, pepper, and Tabasco. Set aside.
- In a large pot, blanche okra for 3 minutes. Drain well. Combine okra with onion and garlic; drizzle dressing over the top of mixture. Marinate in refrigerator 2 hours. Drain and serve.

Yield: 6 servings

Parmesan Pepper Toss

1 small sweet red pepper,
cut into thin strips
1 small bell pepper, cut
into thin strips
1 small purple onion, thinly
sliced and separated into
rings
¼ pound fresh mushrooms,
sliced
1 cup thinly sliced celery
¼ cup olive oil
2 tablespoons chopped
fresh parsley
2 tablespoons red wine
vinegar
½ teaspoon minced garlic
¼ teaspoon salt
¼ teaspoon freshly ground
pepper
Leaf lettuce
½ cup freshly grated
Parmesan cheese

- Combine red pepper, bell pepper, onion, mushrooms, and celery in a large bowl; set aside.
- Combine olive oil, parsley, vinegar, garlic, salt, and pepper; pour over vegetables, tossing gently. Serve in a lettuce-lined dish, and sprinkle with Parmesan cheese.

Yield: 4 to 6 servings

Squash Salad

**5 medium squash, thinly
sliced**
½ cup chopped onion
½ cup chopped bell pepper
½ cup chopped celery

Dressing

2 tablespoons wine vinegar
¼ cup sugar
1 teaspoon salt
½ teaspoon pepper
⅓ cup oil
⅔ cup vinegar
1 clove garlic

• Combine squash, onion, bell
  pepper, and celery in a bowl.
  Set aside.
• In a small bowl or jar,
  combine all Dressing ingredients. Pour over vegetables.
• Chill 12 hours. Drain
  vegetables and serve.

Yield: 8 servings

Bleu Cheese Dressing

2 garlic cloves, peeled
2 cups mayonnaise
1 cup sour cream
**¼ cup chopped fresh
chives**
**2 teaspoons
Worcestershire sauce**
**2 teaspoons fresh lemon
juice**
**½ teaspoon freshly ground
pepper**
**4 ounces bleu cheese,
crumbled**

• Mince garlic in a blender or
  food processor. Blend in
  remaining ingredients except
  the cheese.
• Pour blended ingredients into
  a bowl. Gently stir in bleu
  cheese. Store in a covered
  container in the refrigerator.

Yield: 3 cups

Caesar Salad Dressing

1 large clove garlic
½ cup virgin olive oil
¼ cup grated Parmesan
   cheese
1 egg
1 teaspoon Worcestershire
   sauce
¼ teaspoon coarsely
   ground black pepper
1 teaspoon dry mustard
¾ teaspoon salt
2 tablespoons fresh lemon
   juice

• In a blender, combine garlic and olive oil until thickened.

• Add remaining ingredients; blend until well-mixed.

Yield: Dressing for 2 large bunches leaf lettuce or 2 heads iceberg lettuce.

Celery Seed-Honey Dressing

½ cup sugar
1 teaspoon dry mustard
1 teaspoon paprika
½ teaspoon salt
1 teaspoon celery seed
⅓ cup honey
1 tablespoon lemon juice
4 tablespoons vinegar
1 teaspoon grated onion
1 cup vegetable oil

Note: Great on fresh fruit.

• In a mixing bowl, combine sugar, dry mustard, paprika, salt, and celery seed.

• Add honey, lemon juice, vinegar, and onion. Slowly pour in oil, beating constantly, until thickened.

Yield: 1½ cups

Cole Slaw Dressing

⅓ cup vinegar
1½ cups sugar
1½ teaspoons salt
3 tablespoons prepared
  mustard
3 tablespoons grated onion
3 tablespoons grated bell
  pepper
1 2-ounce jar pimiento
1 cup mayonnaise or
  mayonnaise-type salad
  dressing
Dash of black pepper

• Combine vinegar, sugar,
  and salt, mixing well. Add
  remaining ingredients; stir
  to blend.
• To serve, pour over
  shredded cabbage.

Yield: 1 quart

Note: Keeps well in the refrigerator.

French Dressing

⅓ cup sugar
1 teaspoon salt
1 teaspoon dry mustard
1 teaspoon celery seed
1 teaspoon paprika
1 teaspoon grated onion
4 tablespoons vinegar
1 cup vegetable oil
1 clove garlic, optional

• Mix all ingredients, blending well. Let dressing stand for 1 hour; remove garlic clove, if used, and refrigerate.

Yield: 1½ cups

Note: Excellent over fruit, especially a salad of grapefruit and orange sections with slices of avocado.

Lemon-Garlic Dressing

2 cloves garlic, crushed
1 tablespoon salt
1 teaspoon coarse ground pepper
½ teaspoon dry mustard
3 lemons, juiced
⅓ cup olive oil
⅓ cup vegetable oil

• Combine garlic, salt, pepper, and dry mustard in a shallow bowl. Mash together with a fork until mixture resembles wet sand. Stir in lemon juice until salt dissolves.

• Pour into a small jar; add olive oil and vegetable oil. Shake vigorously to blend all ingredients. Refrigerate.

• Remove from refrigerator at least 1 hour before using on tossed salad.

Yield: 1 cup

Note: Keeps in refrigerator indefinitely.

Artichoke-Capers Salad Dressing

1 16-ounce bottle Italian
dressing
1 4.5-ounce jar sliced
mushrooms, drained
1 3-ounce jar capers,
drained
1 6-ounce jar artichoke
hearts, drained and
chopped
1 10-ounce jar green
olives, chopped
4 tablespoons lemon
pepper
1 tablespoon garlic salt
1 3-ounce jar real bacon
bits
Fresh broccoli flowerets
1 bell pepper, chopped
1 tomato, chopped
Green onions, chopped

• Combine all ingredients and
refrigerate.

Yield: 7 to 8 cups

*Note: Use as a salad dressing over lettuce or pasta. May add or
delete any of the vegetables according to personal taste.*

Breads

B.McWilliams

Cream Cheese Braids

1 8-ounce carton sour
  cream, scalded
½ cup sugar
½ cup butter, melted
1 teaspoon salt
2 packages dry yeast
½ cup warm water
2 eggs, beaten
4 cups all-purpose flour
Filling and Glaze (recipes
  follow)

- Combine scalded sour cream, sugar, butter, and salt; mix well, and cool to lukewarm.
- Dissolve yeast in warm water in a large mixing bowl; stir in sour cream mixture, then eggs. Gradually stir in flour (dough will be soft). Cover tightly; chill overnight.
- Divide dough into 4 equal portions. Turn each portion onto a heavily floured surface; knead 4 or 5 times. Roll each into a 12 by 8-inch rectangle. Spread ¼ of the Filling over each one, leaving a ¼-inch margin around edges. Carefully roll up, jelly-roll fashion, beginning at long side. Firmly pinch edge and ends to seal. Carefully place rolls, seam side down, on greased baking sheets. Make 6 equally spaced X-shaped cuts across top of each loaf. Cover and let rise in a warm place, free from drafts, until doubled in bulk.
- Preheat oven to 375 degrees.
- Bake 15 to 20 minutes. Spread loaves with Glaze while warm.

Yield: 4 12-inch loaves

(Continued on next page)

Cream Cheese Braids *(Continued)*

Filling

**2 8-ounce packages cream
cheese, softened**
¾ cup sugar
1 egg, beaten
⅛ teaspoon salt
2 teaspoons vanilla extract

• Combine all ingredients in
bowl of a processor or in a
mixing bowl. Process in
processor or mix with
electric mixer until well
blended.

Yield: about 2 cups

Glaze (optional)

**2 cups sifted
confectioners' sugar**
¼ cup milk
2 teaspoons vanilla extract

• Combine all ingredients,
mixing well until smooth.

Yield: about 1 cup

Monkey Bread

**3 7½-ounce cans
commercially-prepared
biscuits**
1 cup sugar
2 tablespoons cinnamon
**¼ pound (1 stick) butter,
melted**
1 teaspoon corn syrup

• Preheat oven to 350 degrees.
• Cut biscuits into quarters. In a
mixing bowl, combine sugar
and cinnamon, mixing well.
Roll biscuit quarters in sugar-
cinnamon mixture; place in a
greased Bundt pan.
• Add butter and corn syrup to
remaining sugar-cinnamon
mixture; stir until blended.
Pour over biscuits.
• Bake 20 minutes, or until
golden brown. Immediately
turn onto serving platter.

Yield: 8 servings

Basic Biscuits

2 cups all-purpose flour
2 teaspoons baking powder
¼ teaspoon baking soda
½ teaspoon salt
4 tablespoons butter or shortening
⅔ cup buttermilk, more or less

- Preheat oven to 450 degrees.
- Sift together the flour, baking powder, baking soda, and salt into a mixing bowl. Cut in butter with a pastry blender or two knives until mixture resembles coarse crumbs. Pour in buttermilk to form a soft dough.
- Roll out dough on a floured surface; cut with biscuit cutter. Place on a lightly greased baking sheet.
- Bake 12 to 15 minutes, or until lightly golden.

Yield: 8 biscuits

Note: Use self-rising flour in place of all-purpose flour, baking powder, baking soda, and salt.

Parmesan Cheese Biscuits

2 tablespoons butter, melted
¼ cup corn oil
1 7.5-ounce can commercially-prepared butter-flavored biscuits
1 cup grated Parmesan cheese
1 tablespoon dried parsley flakes

- Preheat oven to 375 degrees.
- Combine butter and oil. Quarter biscuits; roll in butter mixture until well coated. Mix Parmesan cheese and parsley. Roll butter-coated biscuits in Parmesan mixture. Place biscuits close together on baking sheet.
- Bake 10 to 12 minutes, or until done. Do not overbake.

Yield: 40 biscuits

Rolls

⅓ cup shortening
1¾ cups milk
½ cup sugar
¼ cup warm water
1 package dry yeast
3½ cups self-rising flour,
  divided (may use up to
  4 cups)
Butter, melted

- Combine shortening, milk, and sugar in a saucepan; heat on medium until shortening melts. Cool slightly.
- In a large mixing bowl, combine water and yeast, stirring to mix. Set aside until small bubbles form. Add milk mixture to yeast. Sift in 2½ to 3 cups of the flour, enough so that dough is the consistency of cake batter. Let rise 2 hours.
- Add the remaining 1 cup flour and mix by hand. Dough will not be stiff enough to knead. Cover and refrigerate overnight.
- Roll out dough on lightly floured surface. Cut with cutter and dip in melted butter; place on greased baking sheets. Let rise 1 hour.
- Preheat oven to 400 degrees.
- Bake 10 to 15 minutes, or until golden brown.

Yield: 18 rolls

Sour Cream Cornbread

1 8½-ounce can creamed
   corn
1 cup sour cream
2 eggs, beaten
½ cup vegetable oil
1½ cups cornmeal mix
2 teaspoons baking powder

- Preheat oven to 400 degrees.
- Combine corn, sour cream, eggs, and oil, mixing well.
- In a separate bowl, combine cornmeal and baking powder; stir into corn mixture. Pour into a hot greased 9-inch skillet.
- Bake 30 minutes, or until golden brown.

Yield: 8 servings

Spinach Cornbread

4 eggs, beaten
1 cup cottage cheese
1 onion, finely chopped
1 10-ounce package frozen
   chopped spinach, thawed
   and drained
2 8½-ounce boxes
   cornbread mix

- Preheat oven to 375 degrees.
- Mix all ingredients; pour into a greased 9 by 13-inch pan.
- Bake 30 minutes, or until golden brown.

Yield: 12 servings

Mexican Cornbread

1½ cups cornmeal
¼ cup vegetable oil
2 eggs, beaten
1 teaspoon salt
2 jalapeño peppers, seeded
and chopped
1 cup creamed corn
1 cup sour cream or
buttermilk
3 teaspoons baking powder
1 small onion, finely
chopped
2 tablespoons chopped
bell pepper
1 cup grated sharp cheese

• Preheat oven to 350 degrees.
• In a large bowl, combine cornmeal, oil, eggs, salt, peppers, corn, sour cream, baking powder, onion, and bell pepper, stirring well to mix. Pour ½ of the mixture into a hot greased 9-inch skillet or 9 by 9-inch baking pan; sprinkle with ½ of the cheese. Add remaining cornmeal mixture; sprinkle with remaining cheese.
• Bake 35 to 40 minutes, or until golden brown.

Yield: 8 to 9 servings

Note: If using self-rising cornmeal, reduce baking powder to 2 teaspoons.

Broccoli Cornbread

1 10-ounce package chopped
frozen broccoli, thawed
1 large onion, chopped
1 12-ounce carton cottage
cheese
¼ pound (1 stick) butter,
melted
4 eggs, beaten
¾ teaspoon salt
2 8½-ounce boxes
cornbread mix

• Preheat oven to 400 degrees.
• Combine broccoli, onion, cottage cheese, butter, eggs, and salt; add cornbread mix, stirring just until moistened. Pour into a generously greased 9 by 13-inch baking pan.
• Bake 25 minutes, or until golden brown.

Yield: 12 servings

Southern Cornbread

¾ **cup plain cornmeal**
1 cup buttermilk, divided
½ **teaspoon salt**
½ **teaspoon sugar**
1 egg, beaten
½ **teaspoon baking soda**
½ **teaspoon baking powder**
1 teaspoon warm water
1 tablespoon melted
  shortening or vegetable
  oil

- Preheat oven to 425 degrees.
- In a bowl, combine cornmeal with ½ cup of the buttermilk. Mix in salt and sugar. Add egg, stirring just until blended; do not overstir. Pour in the remaining ½ cup buttermilk; stir.
- Pour shortening or oil into a heavy 8-inch skillet. Place skillet in oven until sizzling hot.
- In a small bowl, combine soda, baking powder, and water, stirring until dissolved. Just before baking, add to cornmeal mixture. (If allowed to stand after soda is added, the soda will begin to act too quickly, and the bread will not be light.)
- Remove skillet from oven; pour most of the hot oil into the batter, stirring gently until mixed. Pour batter immediately back into skillet.
- Bake 15 to 20 minutes, or until golden brown.

Yield: 8 servings

Note: May also be made in muffin pans.

Zesty Lemon Muffins

1¾ cups all-purpose flour
¾ cup sugar
1 tablespoon grated lemon
  zest
1 teaspoon baking powder
¾ teaspoon baking soda
¼ teaspoon salt
1 8-ounce carton lemon
  yogurt
6 tablespoons unsalted
  butter, melted
1 large egg, room
  temperature
1 tablespoon fresh lemon
  juice

• Preheat oven to 400 degrees.
• In a large bowl, combine flour, sugar, zest, baking powder, baking soda, and salt, making a well in the center.
• In a separate bowl, whisk together yogurt, butter, egg, and lemon juice. Pour yogurt mixture into well in dry ingredients; stir until just blended. Batter will be lumpy. Spoon into 12 greased muffin cups.
• Bake 20 minutes, or until golden brown. Remove from oven; pierce 6 to 8 holes into each muffin. Coat with hot Lemon Glaze.

Yield: 12 muffins

Lemon Glaze

⅓ cup fresh lemon juice
¼ cup sugar
2 teaspoons grated lemon
  zest

• In a small non-aluminum saucepan, combine all ingredients; cook over low heat until sugar is dissolved.

Orange Muffins

⅓ cup shortening
1 cup sugar
2 eggs
½ teaspoon orange or
  lemon extract
⅓ cup orange juice
⅓ cup water
2 cups flour
2 teaspoons baking powder
½ teaspoon salt
¾ cup chopped pecans

• Preheat oven to 375 degrees.
• In a mixing bowl, combine shortening and sugar; cream together until well blended. Add eggs and extract, stirring to blend. Pour in orange juice and water; stir.
• Sift together the flour, baking powder, and salt. Add to shortening mixture, stirring until just blended. Gently fold in pecans. Pour into 18 greased muffin cups.
• Bake 20 minutes.

Yield: 1½ dozen

Spice Muffins

1 cup butter, softened
2 cups sugar
2 eggs
2 cups unsweetened
  applesauce
3 teaspoons ground
  cinnamon
2 teaspoons ground
  allspice
1 teaspoon ground cloves
1 teaspoon salt
2 teaspoons baking soda
4 cups all-purpose flour
1 cup chopped nuts,
  optional

• Preheat oven to 350 degrees.
• Cream butter and sugar; add eggs. Stir in applesauce, mixing well. Add cinnamon, allspice, cloves, salt, and baking soda.
• Gradually add flour, stirring after each addition. Pour into greased muffin cups.
• Bake 18 to 20 minutes. Batter keeps well in refrigerator until needed.

Yield: 3 dozen

Hushpuppies

1½ cups all-purpose
  yellow cornmeal
½ cup all-purpose flour
2 teaspoons baking
  powder
1 teaspoon sugar
½ teaspoon salt
1 egg, beaten
¾ cup milk
¼ cup minced onion
1 bunch green onion tops,
  finely minced
Vegetable oil

• Combine cornmeal, flour,
  baking powder, sugar, and
  salt in a bowl. Stir in egg,
  milk, onion, and green onion
  tops.
• Drop by rounded teaspoonfuls into oil heated to
  365 degrees; fry until golden
  brown. Drain well. Serve
  immediately.

Yield: 4 to 6 servings

Garlic Cheese Bread

½ pound (2 sticks) butter,
  softened
¼ cup Parmesan cheese
2 tablespoons dried parsley
1 teaspoon celery seed
1 teaspoon garlic powder
1 loaf French bread, halved
  lengthwise

• Preheat oven to 350 degrees.
• Combine butter, Parmesan
  cheese, parsley, celery seed,
  and garlic powder. Spread on
  bread halves. Place on baking
  sheet.
• Bake 10 minutes, or until
  lightly toasted.

Yield: 8 servings

117

Cheese French Bread

¼ pound (1 stick) butter,
softened
½ cup mayonnaise
2 cups grated mozzarella
cheese
½ cup chopped green
onions
1 2¼-ounce can black
olives, drained and
chopped
1 teaspoon garlic powder
1 loaf French bread, halved
lengthwise

• Preheat oven to 350 degrees.
• Combine butter, mayonnaise,
cheese, onion, olives, and
garlic powder. Spread evenly
over bread. (Bread may be
refrigerated at this point until
ready to bake.)
• Bake 10 minutes, or until
cheese melts. Serve hot.

Yield: 8 servings

Cranberry Nut Bread

3 cups all-purpose flour
4 teaspoons baking powder
1 teaspoon salt
1 cup sugar
Grated peel of 1 orange
1 egg, beaten
1 cup milk
2 tablespoons butter,
melted
1¼ cups sliced cranberries
1 cup chopped nuts

• Preheat oven to 350 degrees.
• Sift together the flour, baking
powder, salt, and sugar into a
small bowl; add grated orange
peel.
• In a separate bowl, combine
egg, milk, and butter. Gradually stir in flour mixture. Fold
in cranberries and nuts. Pour
into a greased and floured
5 by 9-inch loaf pan.
• Bake 1 hour. Cool thor-
oughly; wrap in foil and
refrigerate before slicing.

Yield: 1 loaf

*Note: This bread makes delicious sandwiches with butter or
creamed cheese filling.*

Banana Bread

1 cup vegetable oil
2 cups sugar
4 eggs
2 teaspoons soda
⅔ cup buttermilk
1 cup whole-wheat flour
2 cups all-purpose flour
4 large, very ripe bananas,
  mashed
Cream Cheese Icing,
  optional

- Preheat oven to 350 degrees.
- Cream oil and sugar; beat in eggs, adding one at a time and beating well after each addition.
- In a separate small bowl, mix soda with buttermilk. Add to creamed mixture alternately with flours. Stir in bananas and blend thoroughly. Pour into 3 greased and floured 5 by 9-inch loaf pans.
- Bake 45 minutes. Cool 5 to 10 minutes in pans; remove from pans and cool thoroughly on wire racks. Frost with Cream Cheese Icing, if desired.

Yield: 3 loaves

Note: Freezes well.

Cream Cheese Icing

1 8-ounce package cream
  cheese, softened
¼ pound (1 stick) butter,
  softened
1 16-ounce box
  confectioners' sugar
½ teaspoon vanilla extract

- Combine all ingredients, beating until smooth. Any extra icing may be refrigerated up to 3 months in covered container.

Zucchini Bread

3 eggs
1 cup vegetable oil
1½ cups sugar
3 cups grated unpeeled
raw zucchini
3 cups flour
1 teaspoon baking soda
¼ teaspoon baking powder
1 teaspoon salt
3 teaspoons cinnamon
½ cup chopped nuts
3 teaspoons vanilla extract

- Preheat oven to 325 degrees.
- In a large bowl, combine eggs, oil, and sugar, mixing until frothy. Stir in grated zucchini.
- Sift together the flour, baking soda, baking powder, salt, and cinnamon into a separate bowl; add to egg mixture, stirring until blended. Add nuts and vanilla. Pour into 2 greased and floured 5 by 9-inch loaf pans.
- Bake 1 hour. Remove from oven; cool 10 minutes. Remove from pans and cool thoroughly on wire racks.

Yield: 2 loaves

Cinnamon Rolls

1 package dry yeast
1¼ cups lukewarm water
⅓ cup sugar (may use up
  to ½ cup)
1 teaspoon salt
1 egg
½ cup shortening, softened
4 cups sifted all-purpose
  flour, plus more for
  rolling out rolls

Filling

Butter, softened
¼ cup cinnamon
½ cup sugar

Syrup

½ cup firmly packed light
  brown sugar
2 tablespoons butter,
  melted
1 tablespoon water
Raisins, optional
Nuts, optional

- Dissolve yeast in water in large bowl. Add sugar, salt, egg, shortening, and flour. Cover and let rise 2 hours.
- Punch down dough; roll out dough on generously floured surface into 8 by 12-inch rectangle. (Dough will be sticky; may take another cup flour to roll them out.)
- For Filling, spread softened butter over dough. Combine cinnamon and sugar in a small bowl; sprinkle over buttered dough. Roll dough from long side; slice into rolls.
- To make Syrup, combine brown sugar, butter, and water in a small saucepan. Bring to a boil; boil 1 minute. Pour into a 9 by 13-inch baking pan in which raisins and nuts have been added, if using. Place sliced rolls on syrup. Let rise until doubled in bulk.
- Preheat oven to 350 degrees.
- Bake 20 to 25 minutes, or until golden brown.

Yield: 12 to 16 rolls

Easy Whole Wheat Bread

Shortening
3 cups whole-wheat flour,
divided
¼ cup sugar
1 tablespoon salt
2 packages dry yeast
2½ cups milk
¼ cup vegetable oil
1 egg
3 to 4 cups all-purpose
flour
Melted butter, optional

- Using solid shortening, generously grease two 5 by 9-inch loaf pans. Set aside.

- Lightly spoon 2 cups of the whole-wheat flour into measuring cup; level off. Combine whole-wheat flour, sugar, salt, and yeast in a large mixing bowl. Heat milk and oil in a saucepan over low heat until very warm (120 to 130 degrees).

- Add egg and warm milk mixture to flour mixture. Beat ½ minute at low speed; scrape down sides of bowl. Beat an additional 3 minutes at medium speed.

- By hand, gradually stir in the remaining 1 cup whole-wheat flour and 3 to 4 cups all-purpose flour to form a soft dough. Knead on floured surface until smooth and elastic (about 1 minute). Place dough in greased 2½-quart bowl. Turn dough to grease all sides. Cover; let rise in warm place (80 to 85 degrees) until doubled in bulk (45 to 60 minutes).

- Punch down dough. Shape into 2 loaves. Place in greased pans. Cover; let rise in warm place 30 to 35 minutes.

- Preheat oven to 350 degrees.

- Bake 40 to 45 minutes, or until loaf sounds hollow when lightly tapped. Remove from pans immediately. Cool on wire racks. Brush top of loaf with melted butter, if desired.

Yield: 2 loaves

Fruits

and

Vegetables

B.McWilliams

Grilled Fruit Kabobs

¾ cup pineapple juice
¼ cup firmly packed light
brown sugar
¼ teaspoon ground nutmeg
2 cups fresh pineapple
chunks
16 fresh cherries (about
4 ounces)
2 fresh peaches, cut into
wedges
1 large banana, cut into
chunks
Cream cheese, softened
Gingersnaps

- Combine pineapple juice, brown sugar, and nutmeg in a shallow dish.
- Thread fruit onto skewers, and place in juice mixture. Cover; chill 30 minutes.
- Remove kabobs from marinade, discarding marinade.
- Grill, covered with grill lid, over low heat (under 300 degrees) 3 minutes on each side or until lightly browned. Serve with cream cheese and gingersnaps.

Yield: 4 servings

Pineapple Casserole

1 15½-ounce can crushed
pineapple or 1 20-ounce
can pineapple chunks
3 tablespoons all-purpose
flour
½ cup sugar
½ cup grated Cheddar
cheese
4 tablespoons (½ stick)
butter, melted
1 cup crushed round
buttery crackers

- Preheat oven to 350 degrees.
- Drain pineapple and reserve 3 tablespoons juice; mix juice with flour and sugar to make a paste. Stir in drained pineapple and cheese.
- Pour into a greased 9 by 9-inch baking dish. Combine the butter and cracker crumbs; spoon onto top of casserole.
- Bake 20 to 30 minutes.

Yield: 4 to 6 servings

Apple Rings

2 tablespoons oil
⅓ cup plus 3 tablespoons
  sugar
3 apples, washed, cored,
  and sliced
1 cup water

- In skillet, combine oil and 3 tablespoons of the sugar over medium-high heat and caramelize.

- Place sliced apples in skillet with caramelized sugar. Immediately add remaining ⅓ cup sugar and water.

- Cook until apples are transparent and juice has cooked low enough for large bubbles to form.

- Remove apples carefully to a shallow serving dish.

Yield: 3 servings

Note: This is delicious with ham, sausage, eggs, and biscuits.

Baked Beans

½ pound ground beef
1 small bell pepper,
  chopped
1 small onion, chopped
1 31-ounce can pork and
  beans
5 tablespoons thick cane
  syrup
2 tablespoons prepared
  mustard
7 ounces ketchup
1 tablespoon liquid smoke

- Preheat oven to 300 degrees.

- In a large skillet, sauté ground meat, bell pepper, and onion; cook until meat is browned and onions are clear.

- In a separate bowl, combine the beans, syrup, mustard, ketchup, and liquid smoke. Stir in meat mixture. Pour into a greased 9 by 9-inch baking dish.

- Bake 1 hour.

Yield: 10 servings

Desert Beans

8 slices bacon, cut into
2-inch pieces
1 small jalapeño pepper
2 medium yellow onions,
julienned
2 tablespoons vegetable oil
2 tablespoons cider vinegar
1 31-ounce can pork and
beans
⅓ cup ketchup
2 tablespoons prepared
mustard
2 tablespoons
Worcestershire sauce
Dash of Tabasco
½ teaspoon salt
½ teaspoon red pepper
½ cup brown sugar

- Preheat oven to 375 degrees.
- Sauté bacon until halfway done (still limp, not crisp and oily).
- Grill whole jalapeño pepper over hot coals until charred on the outside, or bake at 500 degrees 10 minutes, or until roasted; place into a plastic bag and allow to sit for 15 minutes. Peel, seed, and chop fine, like a paste.
- Sauté onion in oil for 4 to 5 minutes; add cider vinegar and reduce for 3 minutes.
- In a large mixing bowl, combine the bacon, jalapeño pepper, onion, and remaining ingredients, mixing thoroughly.
- Bake 45 minutes.

Yield: 10 servings

Jeff Blackmon
Corporate Chef
Memphis, Tennessee

Asparagus Casserole

1 10¾-ounce can cream of
  mushroom soup
1 10¾-ounce can cream of
  celery soup
3 10½-ounce cans green
  asparagus, drained,
  reserving juice
1 clove fresh garlic,
  minced, or dash of garlic
  powder
3 to 4 dashes Tabasco
1 teaspoon Worcestershire
  sauce
Salt
Pepper
1 teaspoon sugar
4 hard-boiled eggs, sliced,
  optional
Cracker crumbs
2 tablespoons butter
1 14-ounce can artichoke
  hearts, finely chopped
Grated cheese
Toasted slivered almonds

- Preheat oven to 350 degrees.
- Mix soups, reserved asparagus juice, garlic, Tabasco, Worcestershire sauce, salt and pepper to taste, and sugar. Set aside.
- In a 9 by 13-inch greased baking dish, alternate layers of asparagus, eggs if desired, cracker crumbs, soup mixture, and butter; end with artichoke hearts on top. Sprinkle with grated cheese and toasted almonds.
- Bake 25 to 30 minutes, or until bubbly.

Yield: 10 to 12 servings

Asparagus Delight

3 15-ounce cans asparagus
spears
3 tablespoons butter
3 tablespoons all-purpose
flour
1 cup milk
⅛ teaspoon salt
¼ teaspoon white pepper
6 hard-boiled eggs, sliced
2 3-ounce cans mushroom
stems and pieces,
drained
1 cup grated Cheddar
cheese
6 slices bacon, cooked and
crumbled or real bacon
bits
2 tablespoons fine, dry
breadcrumbs

- Preheat oven to 325 degrees.
- Drain asparagus, reserving
1 cup liquid; set aside.
- Melt butter in heavy saucepan
over low heat; add flour,
stirring until smooth. Cook
1 minute, stirring constantly.
Gradually add 1 cup
asparagus liquid and milk;
cook over medium heat,
stirring constantly, until
thickened and bubbly. Stir in
salt and pepper.
- Spread ¼ cup sauce in a
greased 6 by 10-inch baking
dish. Layer half each of the
asparagus, eggs, mushrooms,
cheese, bacon, and sauce.
Repeat layers; sprinkle with
breadcrumbs.
- Bake for 20 to 25 minutes or
until bubbly.

Yield: 8 servings

Horseradish Green Beans

3 14½-ounce cans whole
green beans
1 large onion, sliced or
2 tablespoons dried
minced onion
2 slices bacon, halved
1 cup mayonnaise
1 heaping tablespoon
prepared horseradish
1½ teaspoons dried
parsley flakes
1 teaspoon Worcestershire
sauce
½ teaspoon garlic salt
½ teaspoon onion salt
2 hard-boiled eggs,
chopped
1 lemon, juiced
(3 tablespoons juice)
Salt
Pepper
Celery salt

- Cook beans with onion and bacon 30 minutes; drain well, discarding bacon. Place into a mixing bowl.
- In a separate bowl, combine remaining ingredients; spoon over beans, mixing well. Refrigerate 2 hours to allow flavors to blend.

Yield: 10 to 12 servings

Note: Good served hot or cold.

Sweet and Sour Green Beans

2 16-ounce cans French-
style seasoned green
beans, drained
1 onion, sliced
1 8-ounce can sliced water
chestnuts, drained
6 tablespoons vinegar
5 tablespoons sugar
6 to 8 slices bacon,
cooked and crumbled,
reserving drippings

• Layer beans, onion slices,
and water chestnuts in a 9 by
13-inch baking dish.
• Combine vinegar, sugar, and
bacon drippings; pour over
beans. Sprinkle with
crumbled bacon. Cover and
marinate in refrigerator
overnight.
• Preheat oven to 350 degrees.
• Bake, uncovered, 30 minutes.

Yield: 8 to 10 servings

Cheese Broccoli Soufflé

½ cup chopped onion
6 tablespoons butter,
divided
2 tablespoons all-purpose
flour
½ cup water
Salt
1 8-ounce jar processed
cheese spread
2 10-ounce packages
frozen chopped broccoli,
thawed and drained
3 eggs, beaten
½ cup cracker crumbs

• Preheat oven to 350 degrees.
• Sauté onion in 4 tablespoons
of the butter. Stir in flour and
water. Cook over low heat
until thickened and boiling.
• Add salt to taste and cheese,
stirring until cheese melts.
Gently mix in broccoli and
eggs until blended.
• Pour into a greased 1½-quart
baking dish. Top with crumbs
and dot with remaining
2 tablespoons butter.
• Bake 30 minutes, or until
bubbly.

Yield: 8 servings

Broccoli and Shrimp Casserole

4 10-ounce packages
   frozen broccoli
Salt
Pepper
2 10¾-ounce cans cream
   of shrimp soup
1 cup sour cream
Dash of Worcestershire
   sauce
1 cup grated cheese
1 6-ounce can shrimp
Dash of Tabasco

- Preheat oven to 350 degrees.
- Cook broccoli until tender. Drain well; season with salt and pepper to taste. Pour into a greased 9 by 13-inch baking dish.
- Combine remaining ingredients in a mixing bowl, stirring until well-blended. Pour over broccoli.
- Bake 30 minutes, or until bubbly.

Yield: 12 servings

Zesty Carrot Bake

1 pound carrots, cut into
   ½-inch slices
2 tablespoons minced
   onion
¾ cup mayonnaise
⅓ cup water
1 tablespoon prepared
   horseradish
¼ teaspoon pepper
½ cup dry bread crumbs
2 tablespoons butter,
   melted
½ cup grated sharp
   Cheddar cheese

- Preheat oven to 350 degrees.
- In a saucepan or in microwave, cook carrots until tender. Place in a 1-quart baking dish; set aside.
- In a small bowl, combine the onion, mayonnaise, water, horseradish, and pepper; mix well. Pour over carrots.
- Combine bread crumbs and butter; sprinkle on top.
- Bake, uncovered, 25 to 30 minutes. Sprinkle with cheese. Return to oven for 2 to 3 minutes, or until cheese is melted.

Yield: 6 servings

Swiss Vegetable Medley

1 16-ounce package frozen broccoli, carrots, and cauliflower
1 10¾ ounce can cream of mushroom soup, undiluted
⅓ cup sour cream
1 cup (4 ounces) shredded Swiss cheese, divided
¼ teaspoon black pepper
1 2.8-ounce can French fried onions, divided

• Thaw and drain vegetables. Combine vegetables, soup, sour cream, ½ cup cheese, pepper, and half of the onions.

• Pour into a buttered 1 quart baking dish. Bake, uncovered, at 350 degrees for 30 minutes.

• Sprinkle with remaining cheese and onion; bake, uncovered, 5 additional minutes.

Yield: 6 servings

Cauliflower Sauté

2 cups fresh cauliflower flowerets
½ cup sliced onion
1 clove garlic, minced
1 tablespoon olive oil
1 cup fresh or frozen snow pea pods
1 sweet red pepper, cut into strips
½ cup sliced fresh mushrooms
1 teaspoon dried oregano
¼ teaspoon salt

• Arrange cauliflower in a steamer basket; place over boiling water. Cover and steam 8 minutes; drain and set aside.

• Cook onion and garlic in olive oil in a large nonstick skillet over medium heat, stirring constantly, until tender. Add cauliflower, snow peas, and remaining ingredients; cook, stirring constantly, until heated.

Yield: 4 servings

Fried Corn

12 ears fresh corn
8 slices bacon, uncooked
½ cup butter
2 to 4 teaspoons sugar
2 teaspoons salt
½ teaspoon pepper

- Cut off tips of corn kernels into a large bowl; scrape milk and remaining pulp from cob with a paring knife. Set aside.
- Cook bacon in a large skillet until crisp; remove bacon, reserving 2 tablespoons drippings in skillet. Crumble bacon and set aside. Add corn, butter, and remaining ingredients to skillet.
- Cook over medium heat 20 minutes, stirring frequently. Spoon corn mixture into a serving dish, and sprinkle with crumbled bacon.

Yield: 12 servings

Corn Pudding

2 15-ounce cans creamed corn
3 eggs, beaten
6 tablespoons butter, melted
2 cups cracker crumbs
½ bell pepper, chopped
1 pimiento, chopped
Salt
Pepper
1 medium onion, grated

- Preheat oven to 400 degrees.
- Combine all ingredients, mixing well. Pour into a greased 2-quart baking dish.
- Bake 25 minutes, or until set.

Yield: 6 to 8 servings

133

Skillet Corn Casserole

**12 slices bacon, cut into
  1-inch pieces**
1 cup chopped onion
½ cup chopped bell pepper
**2 tablespoons chopped
  pimiento**
2 eggs, beaten
½ teaspoon salt
¼ teaspoon pepper
**2 15-ounce cans creamed
  corn**
**1 15-ounce can whole
  kernel corn, drained**

• Fry bacon until crisp. Remove and drain well, reserving 2 teaspoons drippings.

• Sauté onion and bell pepper in reserved bacon drippings until tender.

• In a separate bowl, combine remaining ingredients; mix well.

• Pour corn mixture into skillet; cook over low heat 10 minutes. Stir in crumbled bacon. Serve immediately.

Yield: 10 to 12 servings

Eggplant Casserole

**1 quart frozen tomatoes or
1 28-ounce can tomatoes**
½ cup chopped onion
Garlic, minced
Salt
Pepper
**4 eggplants, peeled and
sliced ¼-inch thick**
Vegetable oil
5 to 7 hard-boiled eggs
**8 ounces mozzarella
cheese, grated**
Parmesan cheese

• In a saucepan, combine
tomatoes, onion, garlic to
taste, salt, and pepper; mix
well. Simmer 30 minutes, or
until reduced. Set aside.

• Preheat oven to 350 degrees.

• Season eggplant slices with
salt and pepper to taste.
Brown eggplant in a skillet
in hot oil on both sides;
drain well.

• In a greased 9 by 13-inch
baking dish, spoon a thin
layer of tomato mixture,
followed by layers of the
eggplant slices, boiled eggs,
and cheese. End with tomato
mixture. Sprinkle with
Parmesan cheese.

• Bake, uncovered, 30 minutes, or until bubbly.

Yield: 10 to 12 servings

Eggplant Parmigiana

1 medium eggplant, peeled
and sliced in ¼-inch
slices
5 large eggs
7 cloves garlic, minced
1 cup Parmesan/Romano
cheese (may use more if
desired), divided
¼ cup Italian parsley,
chopped
Salt
Pepper
Seasoned all-purpose flour
Vegetable oil
20 ounces tomato sauce,
divided
8 ounces grated mozzarella
cheese

- Preheat oven to 375 degrees.
- To prepare batter for egg-plant, combine eggs, garlic, cheese, parsley, salt, and pepper to taste in a bowl; blend well.
- Dredge eggplant slices in seasoned flour; dip in batter, and fry in hot oil, cooking until golden brown on both sides; drain well.
- Spoon small amount of tomato sauce onto bottom of 4 greased individual baking dishes; top with eggplant slice on each. Sprinkle with Parmesan/Romano. Top with more tomato sauce and another eggplant slice, ending with another layer of sauce. Sprinkle again with Parmesan/Romano, and end with a sprinkle of mozzarella cheese.
- Bake until hot and cheese is melted with a slight browning.

Yield: 4 servings

Anthony Seta
Certified Master Chef
Memphis, Tennessee

Creole Eggplant

6 medium eggplants
3 medium onions, chopped
5 or 6 green and red bell
  peppers
2 4-ounce cans sliced
  mushrooms
3 cups chopped tomatoes
Salt
Pepper
2 tablespoons
  Worcestershire sauce
Garlic powder
Celery salt
Parmesan cheese

- Peel and dice eggplant. Cook in salted water until tender. Drain in colander.
- Sauté onion, peppers, and mushrooms in butter until tender. Add tomatoes, garlic powder, celery salt, and eggplant. Cook to reduce liquid.
- Preheat oven to 350 degrees.
- Place in greased 9 by 13-inch baking dish. Top with Parmesan cheese. Bake for 35 to 40 minutes.

Yield: 12 to 15 servings

Hominy Casserole

3 tablespoons butter
1 small onion, chopped
½ bell pepper, chopped
3 tablespoons all-purpose
  flour
2 teaspoons prepared
  mustard
Salt
Pepper
1½ cups milk
½ cup grated cheese
1 cup chopped ripe olives
1 29-ounce can white
  hominy

- Preheat oven to 375 degrees.
- Melt butter in skillet, and sauté onion and bell pepper for 5 minutes on low heat. Add flour, mustard, salt and pepper to taste, and milk. Cook until thickened.
- Add cheese, ripe olives, and hominy. Pour into a greased 8 by 8-inch baking dish.
- Bake 25 minutes, or until bubbly.

Yield: 6 servings

137

Chili Pepper Grits Casserole

¾ cup quick grits (not
  instant grits)
3 cups boiling water
½ cup butter, melted
8 ounces grated sharp
  Cheddar cheese
1 4.5-ounce can chopped
  green chili peppers
1 teaspoon salt
½ teaspoon Worcestershire
  sauce
½ teaspoon garlic salt
2 eggs, beaten

- Preheat oven to 350 degrees.
- Cook grits in water according to package directions, stirring often to prevent lumps; remove from heat.
- Stir in remaining ingredients. Pour into a greased 8 by 11-inch baking dish.
- Bake 1 hour, or until set.

Yield: 8 servings

Note: Good with game.

Grilled Onions

4 large Vidalia onions
4 tablespoons butter,
  divided
4 beef bouillon cubes
Salt
Pepper

- Remove skins from onions; wash and core. Place 1 teaspoon butter and 1 bouillon cube in center of each onion. Sprinkle with salt and pepper to taste. Wrap each onion in double thickness of heavy-duty aluminum foil.
- Grill about 45 minutes or bake in a 350 degree oven about 45 minutes.

Yield: 4 servings

Note: May freeze leftover onions in zip-top plastic bag to use later.

Garden Grill

1 **Portobello mushroom,**
   sliced
1 **large onion, thickly sliced**
2 **bell peppers, cut into**
   chunks
4 **yellow squash, thickly**
   sliced
2 **zucchini squash, thickly**
   sliced
1 **large eggplant, peeled**
   and cut into chunks

• Marinate vegetables for
  30 to 40 minutes. Drain and
  place in oiled vegetable grill
  pan. Cook over medium
  coals until tender, brushing
  with Marinade.

Marinade

¾ **cup olive oil**
3 **tablespoons lemon juice**
3 **tablespoons chopped**
   parsley
1 **teaspoon salt**
½ **teaspoon pepper**
2 **cloves garlic, sliced**

• Combine all ingredients and
  pour over vegetables.

Yield: 4 to 6 servings

English Pea Casserole

1 medium onion, chopped
2 tablespoons chopped bell
  pepper
1 cup chopped celery
¼ pound (1 stick) butter
2 15-ounce cans English
  peas, drained
1 8-ounce can sliced water
  chestnuts, drained
1 10¾-ounce can cream of
  mushroom soup
1 2-ounce jar diced
  pimientos, drained
Buttered cracker crumbs

• Preheat oven to 350 degrees.
• In a skillet, sauté onion, pepper, and celery in butter over moderate heat until limp.
• Add remaining ingredients, mixing well. Pour into a greased 2-quart baking dish. Top with cracker crumbs.
• Bake 30 minutes, or until bubbly.

Yield: 6 servings

Baked Potato Salad

4 cups quartered unpeeled
  small red potatoes
1 cup mayonnaise-type
  salad dressing
8 slices bacon, chopped,
  crisply cooked
2 hard-boiled eggs,
  chopped
¼ cup sliced green onions
¼ teaspoon salt
¼ teaspoon pepper

• Preheat oven to 425 degrees.
• Place potatoes on a greased 10 by 15-inch baking pan. Bake 30 to 35 minutes, or until potatoes are tender and golden brown, stirring once.
• Mix salad dressing, bacon, eggs, onions, salt, and pepper in a large bowl. Add potatoes; mix lightly. Serve warm or chilled.

Yield: 6 servings

Creamy Chive-Stuffed Potatoes

8 medium baking potatoes
Vegetable oil
¼ pound (1 stick) butter,
  softened
1 2-ounce carton frozen
  chopped chives, thawed
2 tablespoons chopped
  onion
1 16-ounce carton sour
  cream
½ teaspoon salt
¼ teaspoon pepper
Paprika

• Scrub potatoes thoroughly,
  rub skins with oil and wrap in
  foil; bake at 400 degrees for
  1 hour or until done.
• Allow potatoes to cool to
  touch. Slice skin away from
  top of each potato. Carefully
  scoop out pulp, leaving shells
  intact; mash pulp.
• Combine potato pulp, butter,
  chives, onion, sour cream,
  salt, and pepper; mix well.
  Stuff shells with potato
  mixture; sprinkle with
  paprika. Bake potatoes at
  400 degrees for 10 minutes
  or until heated thoroughly.

Yield: 8 servings

Sour Cream Potatoes

8 medium potatoes, cubed
  and cooked
1 8-ounce carton sour
  cream
1 medium onion, finely
  chopped
1 2-ounce jar pimiento,
  drained
¼ pound (1 stick) butter
2 cups crushed corn flake
  cereal
1 cup grated cheese
Salt
Pepper

• Preheat oven to 375 degrees.
• Mash potatoes; stir in sour
  cream, onion, and pimiento.
  Spoon into a greased 9 by
  13-inch baking dish.
• Top with several pats of
  butter, crushed cereal, and
  cheese.
• Bake 30 minutes, or until
  bubbly.

Yield: 8 to 10 servings

Picnic Potato Salad

8 potatoes, peeled, diced,
and cooked
4 hard-boiled eggs, finely
chopped
4 green onions, finely
chopped
2 slices crisp bacon,
crumbled
1 large dill pickle, finely
chopped
1 tablespoon pickle juice
½ small bell pepper, finely
chopped
Salt
Pepper
4 heaping tablespoons
mayonnaise or salad
dressing
1 tablespoon mustard

• Combine potatoes, eggs,
green onion, bacon, dill
pickle, juice, bell pepper, salt
and pepper in a large mixing
bowl.

• In a separate small bowl, stir
together the mayonnaise and
mustard; spoon over potato
mixture and gently mix
together.

Yield: 15 servings

Spinach Casserole

2 10-ounce packages
chopped spinach
3 tablespoons butter,
melted
1 teaspoon Worcestershire
sauce
Salt
Pepper
1 4-ounce jar mushroom
slices
¼ cup chopped onion
¼ cup milk
1 cup grated cheese

- Preheat oven to 350 degrees.
- Cook spinach according to package directions. Squeeze out excess liquid.
- Add remaining ingredients, mixing well. Pour into a greased 9 by 9-inch baking dish.
- Bake 30 minutes.

Yield: 4 servings

Spinach-Sour Cream Casserole

1 10-ounce package frozen
chopped spinach
1 tablespoon minced onion
or 1 teaspoon dried
minced onion
2 eggs
½ cup sour cream
1 cup grated Parmesan
cheese
1 tablespoon all-purpose
flour
2 tablespoons butter,
melted
Salt
Pepper

- Preheat oven to 350 degrees.
- Cook spinach according to package directions with the onion; drain. Set aside.
- In a separate mixing bowl, combine the remaining ingredients, mixing well. Stir in spinach. Pour into a greased 1½-quart baking dish.
- Bake 25 to 30 minutes, or until center is set. Do not overcook.

Yield: 4 servings

Plantation Squash

**10 cups sliced squash,
cooked and mashed**
1 cup chopped onion
**½ cup chopped red bell
pepper**
**½ cup chopped green bell
pepper**
2 eggs
½ cup butter
2 tablespoons sugar
1½ teaspoons salt
1 cup grated cheese
½ teaspoon red pepper
**1 tablespoon
Worcestershire sauce**
**1½ teaspoons garlic
powder**
1½ cups mayonnaise
Bread crumbs

- Sauté onions and peppers until tender. Add to mashed squash and all other ingredients, except bread crumbs. Mix well and place in a buttered 9 by 13-inch baking dish. Top with bread crumbs.
- Bake at 350 degrees for 30 minutes.

Yield: 10 servings

Squash Dressing

½ cup chopped onion
½ cup chopped bell pepper
½ cup chopped celery
¼ cup (½ stick) butter
2 cups corn bread crumbs
2 cups squash, cooked and
   mashed
2 eggs, well beaten
1 10¾-ounce cream of
   chicken or cream of
   celery soup, undiluted
Seasonings to taste
   Salt
   Black pepper
   Red pepper
   Sage
   Nutmeg

- Sauté onion, bell pepper, and celery in butter. Add vegetables to cornbread and squash. Blend in eggs, soup, and add seasonings as you desire.
- Place in a well greased 9 by 13-inch baking dish. Bake at 350 degrees for about 20 minutes; or until hot and bubbly.

Yield: 12 servings

Note: May freeze and bake later.

145

Italian Zucchini Crescent Pie

**4 cups thinly-sliced
unpeeled zucchini
1 cup coarsely chopped
onion
¼ pound (1 stick) butter
½ cup chopped fresh
parsley or ¼ cup dried
parsley
½ teaspoon salt
½ teaspoon pepper
¼ teaspoon garlic powder
¼ teaspoon basil leaves
¼ teaspoon oregano leaves
2 eggs, beaten
8 ounces (2 cups) grated
Munster or mozzarella
cheese
1 8-ounce can refrigerated
crescent rolls
2 teaspoons Dijon mustard**

- Preheat oven to 375 degrees.
- In a 10-inch skillet, cook zucchini and onion in butter until tender, about 10 minutes. Stir in parsley, salt, pepper, garlic powder, basil, and oregano.
- In a large bowl, blend eggs and cheese. Stir in vegetable mixture.
- Separate crescent rolls into 8 triangles and place in an ungreased 11-inch quiche pan, 10-inch pie pan, or 8 by 12-inch baking dish. Press over bottom and up sides to form a crust.
- Spread crust with mustard. Pour vegetable mixture evenly over crust.
- Bake 18 to 20 minutes, or until knife inserted in center comes out clean. Let stand 10 minutes. Cut into wedges.

Yield: 8 servings

Stuffed Zucchini

**3 zucchini, halved, pulp
removed and reserved
1 onion, chopped
1 bell pepper, chopped
1 clove garlic, crushed
¼ pound (1 stick) butter
½ pound hot pork sausage
8 ounces Mexican
processed cheese loaf
4 ounces salsa
Dried bread crumbs**

- Preheat oven to 350 degrees.
- Steam zucchini hulls in boiling water until tender. Set aside.
- Chop zucchini pulp; sauté with onion, bell pepper, and garlic in butter.
- In a separate skillet, fry sausage until browned; combine with zucchini mixture. Stir in cheese and salsa. Add enough bread crumbs to thicken mixture.
- Stuff zucchini hulls with sausage mixture. Place in a greased 9 by 13-inch baking dish.
- Bake 30 minutes, or until heated thoroughly.

Yield: 6 servings

Southern Sweet Potatoes

**3 cups cooked sweet
potatoes, mashed
¼ cup milk
½ cup margarine
2 eggs, beaten
1 cup sugar
1 teaspoon vanilla
Marshmallows**

- Preheat oven to 350 degrees.
- Combine all ingredients except marshmallows; place in a heavily buttered 9 by 9-inch baking dish.
- Bake for 30 minutes. Put marshmallows on top and cook until brown.

Yield: 4 to 6 servings

147

Sweet Potato Casserole

3 cups cooked sweet
potatoes, mashed (see
Note)
1 cup sugar
½ teaspoon salt
2 eggs, beaten
4 tablespoons butter,
melted
½ cup milk
½ teaspoon vanilla

Topping

1 cup brown sugar
½ cup all-purpose flour
4 tablespoons butter,
melted
1 cup chopped pecans,
optional
Dash of cinnamon
Dash of allspice

- Preheat oven to 350 degrees.
- Combine sweet potatoes,
  sugar, salt, eggs, butter, milk,
  and vanilla; pour into a
  greased 9 by 9-inch baking
  dish.
- To make Topping, mix
  brown sugar, flour, butter,
  pecans if desired, cinnamon,
  and allspice in a mixing bowl;
  sprinkle over potatoes.
- Bake 30 minutes.

Yield: 4 to 6 servings

Note: Boil whole unpeeled potatoes; peel after cooked.

Italian-Style Tomatoes

4 large firm ripe tomatoes
½ teaspoon salt
½ teaspoon pepper
8 ounces mild Italian sausage
1 cup diced onion
2 tablespoons minced fresh garlic
1½ cups cooked long-grain rice
½ cup freshly grated Parmesan cheese, divided
¼ teaspoon dried crushed red pepper
¼ cup minced fresh parsley
¼ cup sliced almonds
1 large egg, lightly beaten

- Preheat oven to 425 degrees.

- Cut tomatoes in half crosswise; scoop pulp into a bowl, leaving shells intact. Set pulp aside. Sprinkle shells with salt and pepper; place, upside down, on paper towels to drain.

- Remove and discard casings from sausage. Brown sausage in a large skillet over medium heat, stirring until it crumbles; drain.

- Add onion and garlic, and sauté until tender. Add tomato pulp, and cook, stirring often, 15 minutes or until liquid evaporates; cool slightly.

- Stir in rice, ¼ cup of the cheese, and remaining ingredients; spoon into tomato shells, and place in a 9 by 13-inch baking dish. Sprinkle with remaining ¼ cup cheese.

- Bake 20 minutes, or just until lightly browned.

Yield: 8 servings

Tomato Pie

1 deep dish pie crust
Parmesan cheese
Fresh tomatoes, sliced
Italian seasoning
Garlic powder
Swiss cheese, grated
Monterey Jack cheese,
  grated
Butter

- Bake pie crust according to package directions; sprinkle with Parmesan cheese while hot.
- Cool oven to 350 degrees.
- In pie crust, place a layer of tomatoes, sprinkle with Parmesan cheese, Italian seasoning, garlic powder, Swiss cheese, and Monterey Jack cheese. Repeat layers, ending with seasonings and cheese. Dot with butter.
- Bake 20 to 25 minutes, or until cheese is melted and starts to brown. Let stand 10 minutes before cutting.

Yield: 6 servings

Note: A wonderful way to use homegrown tomatoes.

Tomatoes Rockefeller

6 tomatoes, washed and cored
Salt
1 10-ounce package frozen chopped spinach, thawed
4 tablespoons butter
½ cup diced onion
1 clove garlic, minced
½ cup soft bread crumbs
1 teaspoon salt
1 teaspoon chopped fresh thyme
½ cup freshly grated Parmesan cheese
2 large eggs, lightly beaten

- Preheat oven to 350 degrees.
- Cut off tops of tomatoes; scoop out and discard pulp, leaving shells intact. Sprinkle shells lightly with salt; place upside down on paper towels to drain.
- Drain spinach; press between paper towels to remove excess moisture.
- Melt butter in a large skillet; add onion and garlic, and sauté until tender. Stir in spinach and remaining ingredients; cook, stirring constantly, until eggs are set.
- Spoon mixture into tomato shells, and place in 9 by 13-inch baking dish.
- Bake 20 minutes, or just until lightly browned.

Yield: 6 servings

Note: May be used as an appetizer using 1 quart cherry tomatoes and baking for 12 to 15 minutes.

Vegetable Frittata

2 tablespoons olive oil
2 cloves garlic, minced
⅓ cup chopped green
 onions and tops
2 yellow squash, thinly
 sliced
1 large zucchini, thinly
 sliced
1 unpeeled eggplant, thinly
 sliced
½ pound fresh mushrooms,
 thinly sliced
3 eggs
1 teaspoon Italian
 seasoning
1 teaspoon salt
½ teaspoon freshly ground
 pepper
2 cups grated Monterey
 Jack cheese
½ cup freshly grated
 Parmesan cheese

- Preheat oven to 350 degrees.
- In a large skillet, heat the olive oil and sauté garlic until limp; add green onions, squash, zucchini, eggplant, and mushrooms. Sauté, turning and stirring, 7 minutes.
- In a separate bowl, beat eggs until frothy. Add Italian seasoning, salt, and pepper.
- Spoon vegetables into a greased 9 by 13-inch baking dish; pour egg mixture over top. Cover with cheeses.
- Bake 40 minutes, or until set.

Yield: 8 servings

Note: May be made ahead of time and refrigerated until ready to bake. A nice idea for a buffet or for roast chicken, and the amounts can be adjusted to suit any crowd.

Trish Berry
Member IACP
The Good Day Cafe and Catering
Indianola, Mississippi

Pasta

and

Rice

B. McWilliams

Baked Ziti

1 pound ricotta cheese
4 cloves garlic, minced
¼ cup chopped Italian
parsley
¾ cup grated Parmesan/
Romano cheese, divided
1 cup shredded provolone
cheese, divided
1 cup shredded mozzarella
cheese, divided
Salt
Pepper
2 large eggs, beaten
1 pound ziti
48 ounces commercially-
prepared marinara sauce
½ pound Italian sausage,
sautéed and drained

- Preheat oven to 350 degrees.
- Combine the ricotta, garlic, parsley, ½ cup of the Parmesan/Romano cheese, ½ of the provolone, and ½ of the mozzarella in a mixing bowl. Season with salt and pepper to taste. Fold in beaten eggs; set aside.
- Cook ziti according to package directions; drain well. Shock with ice-cold water; drain again completely.
- In a bowl, combine the cooked ziti with 3 cups of the marinara sauce. Set aside.
- Pour ¾ cup of the marinara sauce into a greased 9 by 13-inch baking dish; layer ½ of the sauced ziti into dish, followed by all of the ricotta filling. Sprinkle Italian sausage on top. Cover with remaining ziti. Ladle 1 cup of the remaining marinara sauce over pasta; sprinkle with remaining Parmesan/Romano cheese, and top with remaining provolone and mozzarella cheeses.
- Bake, covered, 45 to 50 minutes; remove cover and continue to bake for an additional 10 to 15 minutes, or until cheese is a light brown. Remove from oven, cover again, and allow to sit for 5 to 10 minutes. Serve each portion topped with a spoonful of remaining heated marinara sauce.

Yield: 8 servings

Anthony Seta
Certified Master Chef
Memphis, Tennessee

Linguini alla Puttanesca

1 pound linguini
⅓ cup fresh shredded basil
6 tablespoons butter
½ cup chopped Italian
  parsley
4 ounces pancetta or bacon
3 ounces olive oil
4 garlic cloves, minced
2 chili peppers
1 medium onion, diced
  small
4 ounces anchovy fillets,
  chopped
5 tablespoons capers
16 black pitted olives
3 cups Italian plum
  tomatoes with juice
Salt
Pepper

• Cook linguini in boiling salted water; drain when al dente (see Note). In a heated bowl, toss pasta with basil, butter, and parsley. Keep warm. Set aside.

• Sauté pancetta or bacon in a heavy duty pot on medium-high heat until light brown and crisp. Drain and set aside.

• Combine olive oil with the bacon drippings; sauté garlic and chili peppers until aroma fills the air. Stir in onion; cook until limp. Add ancho-vies, capers, and olives, stirring well.

• Pour in tomatoes; season with salt and pepper to taste. Bring to a boil and simmer 5 minutes. Stir in cooked pancetta.

• Pile warm linguini onto a serving platter. Pour ¾ of the sauce over the top. Serve immediately with the remain-ing sauce on the side with crusty bread.

Yield: 4 to 6 servings

Note: "Al dente" is an Italian phrase meaning "to the tooth", used to describe pasta or other food that is cooked only until it offers a slight resistance when bitten into, but which is not soft or overdone.

Anthony Seta
Certified Master Chef
Memphis, Tennessee

155

Chicken Pasta Primavera

1 12-ounce package
fettuccine, cooked and
drained
1 pound fresh broccoli, cut
into flowerets (may use
up to 1½ pounds)
2 medium zucchini, thinly
sliced
6 green onions, chopped
1 bell pepper, cut into
slices or strips, or
chopped
1 6-ounce can sliced ripe
olives, drained
2 cups cooked chopped
chicken
1 cup grated Parmesan
cheese
½ teaspoon salt
½ teaspoon freshly ground
pepper

Basil Sauce

½ cup chopped fresh basil
1 clove garlic
2 eggs
½ teaspoon dry mustard
½ teaspoon salt
½ teaspoon lemon juice
2 tablespoons tarragon
wine vinegar
1½ cups vegetable oil
½ cup sour cream

• Combine fettuccine with
broccoli, zucchini, green
onions, bell pepper, olives,
chicken, cheese, salt and
pepper. Set aside.

• To make Sauce, combine
basil and garlic in blender;
process for 30 seconds.
Add eggs, dry mustard, salt,
lemon juice, and vinegar.
Process 20 seconds. With
blender running, gradually
add oil in a slow, steady
stream, mixing just until
well-blended and thickened.
Add sour cream; process
10 additional seconds.

• Top fettuccine mixture with
Sauce. This can be made the
night before; add just enough
sauce to moisten. Refrigerate.
Before serving, add remaining sauce and mix well.

Yield: 10 to 12 servings

Macaroni Salad

1 cup uncooked macaroni
4 strips bacon, cooked and
   crumbled
2 tablespoons minced onion
2 teaspoons lemon juice
¼ cup chopped green pepper
¼ cup chopped stuffed olives
½ cup chopped celery
2 boiled eggs, chopped
½ cup mayonnaise or salad
   dressing
Salad greens
Paprika

- Boil macaroni in salted water until tender. Drain thoroughly; chill in a shallow dish in the refrigerator.
- Combine the remaining ingredients except the salad greens and paprika, being sure to coat all pieces with the dressing.
- Chill for a few hours to allow flavors to blend. Serve on greens. Garnish with paprika.

Yield: 6 servings

Vermicelli Salad

1 16-ounce package
   vermicelli, cooked and
   drained
½ red onion, chopped
½ bell pepper, chopped
2 tomatoes, chopped
1 6-ounce can sliced ripe
   olives

Marinade

1 8-ounce bottle Italian
   dressing
4 tablespoons Salad
   Supreme seasoning
1 0.7-ounce package dry
   Italian dressing mix

- Combine vermicelli, onion, bell pepper, tomatoes, and ripe olives in a large mixing bowl. Set aside.
- In a small bowl or jar with a tight-fitting lid, combine the dressings; mix well.
- Pour dressings over vermicelli mixture, tossing to coat well. Chill overnight.

Yield: 10 to 12 servings

Pasta Chicken Salad

3 cups bow-tie pasta, cooked and drained
3 cups cooked and cubed chicken
¼ cup chopped onion
¼ cup diced celery
1½ cups seedless grapes, halved
1 11-ounce can Mandarin oranges, drained
¾ cup slivered almonds, lightly toasted
1½ cups mayonnaise

• Combine all ingredients in a large mixing bowl.
• Cover tightly and chill for a few hours to allow flavors to blend.

Yield: 10 to 12 servings

Rice and Artichoke Salad

6 cups cooked rice
2 6-ounce jars marinated artichoke hearts, chopped (including juice)
1 bunch green onions, chopped
1 3-ounce jar stuffed olives, sliced
⅔ cup mayonnaise
1 teaspoon curry powder
Salt

• Mix rice, artichoke hearts and juice, green onions, olives, mayonnaise, and curry powder. Season with salt to taste.
• Chill in the refrigerator for a few hours to allow flavors to blend.

Yield: 10 to 12 servings

Consommé Rice

¼ **pound (1 stick) butter, melted**
1 14½-ounce can chicken or beef broth
1 can water
1 cup uncooked rice
½ cup diced bell pepper
½ cup sliced mushrooms
1 small onion, chopped

- Preheat oven to 350 degrees.
- Combine all ingredients in a glass casserole dish.
- Bake for 1 hour, or until liquid is absorbed.

Yield: 6 servings

Lemon Pilaf

2 tablespoons butter
½ cup uncooked regular rice
½ cup uncooked vermicelli, broken in 1-inch pieces
1 14½-ounce can chicken broth
1 tablespoon grated lemon peel
1 tablespoon chopped fresh parsley

- In a medium saucepan, melt butter. Add rice and pasta; stir over medium heat until golden.
- Pour in broth; bring to a boil. Cover and reduce heat. Simmer 15 to 20 minutes or until rice is tender and liquid is absorbed.
- Stir in lemon peel and parsley.

Yield: 4 servings

159

Olive-Rice Casserole

1 cup uncooked rice
1 cup Cheddar cheese,
 diced
1 3-ounce jar stuffed
 olives, sliced
1 cup tomatoes, drained
½ cup chopped onion
¼ cup vegetable oil
1 cup water
Salt
Pepper

- Preheat oven to 350 degrees.
- Combine all ingredients in 2-quart baking dish. Bake, covered, for 1 hour, or until all liquid is absorbed.

Yield: 6 to 8 servings

Sautéed Armenian Rice

¼ pound (1 stick) butter
4 cloves garlic
1 cup vermicelli, broken
1 cup uncooked rice
2 cups chicken broth
1 large bell pepper,
 chopped in large pieces
1 2½-ounce can
 mushrooms, drained
1 6-ounce can whole ripe
 olives, halved
1 8-ounce can sliced water
 chestnuts, drained

- Melt butter in skillet; cook garlic until soft. Remove garlic and discard. Add vermicelli to butter. Sauté until golden brown.
- Stir in remaining ingredients; mix well. Bring to a boil; lower heat to medium-low. Cook, covered, for 20 to 30 minutes.

Yield: 8 servings

Fried Rice

2 tablespoons olive oil,
divided
1 egg, beaten
¼ cup green onions,
chopped
1 4-ounce can sliced
mushrooms
2 cups shrimp, pork, ham,
or sausage
1 14-ounce can bean
sprouts
1 teaspoon salt
1 teaspoon pepper
2 cups cooked rice
1 tablespoon soy sauce
1 tablespoon chicken broth

- Pour 1 tablespoon of the olive oil into a wok or large skillet; stir in egg and scramble. Remove egg from pan and set aside.
- In the same wok, sauté onions and mushrooms in the remaining 1 tablespoon olive oil. Add meat and brown. Move mixture to one side of the pan.
- Stir in bean sprouts, salt, and pepper. Add rice, soy sauce, broth, and cooked egg. Mix well and heat thoroughly. Serve immediately.

Yield: 4 to 6 servings

Note: This is especially good to use with any leftover meat you might have on hand.

Spanish Rice

½ cup chopped onion
½ cup chopped bell pepper
2 tablespoons vegetable oil
1 28-ounce can tomatoes
  and juice
1 cup beef broth
1½ teaspoons salt
1 cup converted rice
½ teaspoon cumin
1 teaspoon sugar
½ teaspoon basil
½ teaspoon oregano
½ pound lean ground beef,
  cooked

- In a skillet, sauté onion and bell pepper in oil until limp. Add tomatoes and juice, broth, and salt. Bring to a boil.
- Stir in rice slowly so as not to disturb boiling. Lower heat; stir in cumin, sugar, basil, and oregano. Cover and simmer 15 minutes.
- Crumble in ground beef and cook until done.

Yield: 8 servings

Note: This is very good on the day it is made, but is even better the second day.

162

Meat

Entrees

B. McWilliams

Mushroom-Garlic Roast

1 5-pound roast
3 cloves garlic, sliced
Salt
Pepper
2 10¾-ounce cans cream
  of mushroom soup
2 1-ounce packages dry
  onion soup mix
1 cup water

- Pierce roast with sharp knife. Insert slivers of garlic in slits. Salt and pepper roast to taste.
- Place roast in Dutch oven. Combine mushroom soup and onion soup mix. Spread over roast.
- Cook, uncovered, in a 350 degree oven for 30 minutes.
- Stir in water and turn roast to other side. Reduce heat to 300 degrees, cover and continue cooking until desired degree of doneness. Add more water for thinning gravy, if needed.

Yield: 10 servings

Coca-Cola Beef Roast

1 4-pound beef roast
1 1-ounce package dry
  onion soup mix
1 12-ounce can cola-
  flavored soft drink

- Place roast in Dutch oven. Sprinkle soup mix over meat; pour cola over top.
- Bake at 350 degrees until desired degree of doneness.

Yield: 8 servings

164

Golden Roast and Gravy

1 4-pound beef roast
Salt
Pepper
All-purpose flour for
  dredging
Vegetable oil
1 10¾-ounce can golden
  mushroom soup
1 10¾-ounce can French
  onion soup, or cream of
  mushroom soup
1 can water
1 large onion, cut in
  chunks
4 medium potatoes, cut in
  chunks
3 carrots, cut in chunks

- Cover roast with salt, pepper, and flour. Brown in a small amount of oil in iron Dutch oven.
- Mix soups and water; add to roast; add onion, and cook on top of stove or in the oven at 350 degrees, for 2½ to 3 hours. During last hour of cooking, add potatoes and carrots.

Yield: 8 servings

Peppered Rib Eye Steaks

¾ teaspoon freshly ground
black pepper
1 teaspoon dried thyme
1½ teaspoons garlic
powder
½ teaspoon salt
½ teaspoon ground red
pepper
½ teaspoon lemon pepper
½ teaspoon dried parsley
flakes
2 rib eye steaks,
1½-inches thick
1 tablespoon olive oil

• Combine black pepper, thyme, garlic powder, salt, red pepper, lemon pepper, and parsley. Brush steaks with oil; rub with pepper mixture. Cover and chill 1 hour.

• Grill, covered with grill lid, over medium-high heat about 10 minutes on each side or to desired degree of doneness.

Yield: 2 servings

Chili Pepper Beef Loaf

2 pounds lean ground beef
2 large eggs
1½ cups salsa, divided
½ cup finely crushed bread
crumbs
½ cup minced onion
1 teaspoon salt
½ teaspoon pepper
1 4-ounce can whole green
chilies
1 cup (4 ounces) grated
Monterey Jack cheese
Sour cream

• Preheat oven to 400 degrees.

• In a bowl, combine ground beef, eggs, ½ cup of the salsa, the bread crumbs, onion, salt, and pepper, mixing well. Press ½ of the ground beef mixture in 5 by 9-inch loaf pan. Slice chilies into ½-inch strips; arrange over meat. Sprinkle with ½ cup of the cheese. Press remaining ground beef mixture over cheese.

• Bake 55 minutes. Drain off excess juice. Sprinkle with the remaining ½ cup cheese. Allow to sit 10 minutes. Slice and serve with the remaining 1 cup salsa and sour cream.

Yield: 6 to 8 servings

Deli-Style Roast Beef

1 4-pound eye of round
    roast
5 cloves garlic, halved
1 8-ounce can tomato
    sauce
1 cup dry red wine
¼ cup Worcestershire
    sauce
¼ cup lemon juice
¼ cup Creole mustard
2 tablespoons hot sauce
2 tablespoons prepared
    horseradish
2 teaspoons onion powder
2 bay leaves
Vegetable cooking spray

- Cut 10 small, deep slits in roast; insert garlic halves into slits. Place in a heavy-duty, zip-lock bag.

- Combine tomato sauce, wine, Worcestershire sauce, lemon juice, mustard, hot sauce, horseradish, onion powder, and bay leaves; reserve ⅓ cup of this marinade mixture. Pour remaining marinade over roast; seal bag. Refrigerate roast and reserved marinade 8 hours.

- Remove roast from marinade, discarding marinade. Place on a rack in a shallow roasting pan coated with cooking spray, and insert meat thermometer. For a rare roast, bake at 325 degrees for 1½ hours or until thermometer reaches 140 degrees, basting several times with ⅓ cup reserved marinade.

- Remove from oven; cool. Wrap roast securely in plastic wrap to retain moisture. Chill several hours before slicing.

Yield: 15 servings

Beef Brisket

1 4-pound fresh beef
brisket (see Note)
½ cup cola-flavored soft
drink
⅓ cup Worcestershire
sauce
½ teaspoon ground
allspice
½ teaspoon chili powder
½ teaspoon garlic powder
½ teaspoon onion powder
½ teaspoon paprika
½ teaspoon seasoned salt
½ teaspoon sugar
¼ teaspoon pepper
½ cup cider vinegar
¼ pound (1 stick) butter,
melted
⅓ cup soy sauce
¾ cup barbecue sauce plus
additional for serving

- Place brisket in a shallow dish. Combine cola and Worcestershire sauce; pour over meat. Cover and refrigerate overnight. Drain meat; discard marinade.

- Combine the allspice, chili powder, garlic powder, onion powder, paprika, seasoned salt, sugar, and pepper; rub over brisket and place in a large shallow roasting pan.

- Combine vinegar, butter and soy sauce; pour over meat. Cover and bake at 325 degrees for 2 hours, basting occasionally. Drain drippings.

- Pour barbecue sauce over meat. Cover and bake for 1 hour or until the meat is tender.

- Remove meat from pan; let stand 15 minutes before slicing. Serve with additional barbecue sauce.

Yield: 8 servings

Note: This is a fresh brisket, not corned beef.

Beef Kabobs

⅓ cup olive oil
¼ cup balsamic vinegar
2 tablespoons soy sauce
1 teaspoon lemon juice
2 tablespoons
  Worcestershire sauce
2 cloves garlic, minced
1 tablespoon Dijon
  mustard
1 teaspoon chopped
  parsley
Salt
Pepper
1½ pounds sirloin beef,
  cubed
1 sweet red pepper
1 sweet yellow pepper
1 large Vidalia onion
1 pint cherry tomatoes
1 pint mushrooms

- To make marinade, combine olive oil, vinegar, soy sauce, lemon juice, Worcestershire sauce, garlic, mustard, parsley, and salt and pepper to taste in small bowl, mixing well to combine.

- Place beef in bowl or glass dish; pour in marinade. Stir so that all beef pieces are well coated. Cover and marinate 1 hour at room temperature.

- Cut peppers and onion into pieces, large enough to place on skewers. Leave tomatoes and mushrooms whole. Alternate beef and vegetables on skewers. Brush with extra marinade.

- Grill over medium-high heat until desired doneness, turning skewers occasionally.

Yield: 4 servings

Beef Kabobs with Seasoned Rice

1 pound sirloin beef, cubed
Beef marinade of choice
1 6-ounce package long-
grain and wild rice mix
1 cup mayonnaise, divided
1 cup cherry tomatoes
1 cup mushroom halves
½ cup bell pepper chunks
2 tablespoons chopped
parsley
2 tablespoons chopped
onion
1 tablespoon milk
¼ teaspoon salt
⅛ teaspoon garlic powder
⅛ teaspoon pepper

- Combine cubed beef and marinade in shallow glass dish; marinate 2 or more hours. Drain beef, discarding marinade.

- Prepare rice according to package directions, omitting margarine. Combine rice and ½ cup of the mayonnaise. Toss lightly. Spoon into 8 by 8-inch baking dish.

- Preheat oven to 350 degrees.

- Alternate marinated beef, tomatoes, mushrooms, and bell pepper on skewers. Arrange over rice.

- Bake 30 minutes, turning kabobs once.

- Combine the remaining ½ cup mayonnaise and the remaining ingredients in small bowl, mixing well. Serve over kabobs.

Yield: 4 servings

Tenderloin Stuffed with Mushrooms

1 5 to 6-pound whole
   tenderloin
1 cup Chablis wine
¼ pound (1 stick) butter
½ cup cognac
1 teaspoon salt
⅛ teaspoon pepper
¼ teaspoon thyme
1 bay leaf
1 small onion, thinly sliced
1 pound fresh mushrooms,
   thinly sliced

• Combine tenderloin and Chablis in shallow glass dish; marinate meat overnight, turning occasionally.

• Melt butter in saucepan; add cognac, salt, pepper, thyme, and bay leaf, stirring well. Add onion slices; cook until reduced by half. Add mushrooms; cook 4 minutes.

• Remove meat from marinade, reserving marinade. Cut a pocket in tenderloin. Stuff with onion mixture. Secure with wooden picks.

• Place reserved marinade in small saucepan. Bring to a boil; boil 3 to 4 minutes.

• Place tenderloin on a spit; roast 1 hour (for rare). Baste with marinade.

Yield: 8 servings

Note: Tenderloin may be roasted in a 475 degree oven 25 minutes.

Filet Mignon with Tomato and Artichoke Sauce

2 1¼-inch thick filet
   mignon steaks
Beef marinade of choice
½ cup oil-packed dried
   tomatoes
1½ tablespoons finely
   chopped green onions
1 clove garlic, finely
   chopped
1 14-ounce can artichoke
   hearts, drained and
   quartered
¼ teaspoon dried basil

- Place steaks in 8-inch square dish; pour marinade over steaks; cover and chill 8 hours, turning steaks several times. Drain, discarding marinade.

- Grill, uncovered, over medium-hot coals (350 to 400 degrees) 4 to 5 minutes on each side, or until desired degree of doneness. Keep warm.

- Drain 1 tablespoon oil from tomatoes, and place in large skillet. Chop tomatoes and set aside. Cook green onions and garlic in reserved oil in skillet over medium-high heat, stirring constantly, 2 minutes. Add tomatoes, artichoke hearts, and basil; cook 5 minutes, stirring frequently. Thinly slice steaks; serve with tomato mixture.

Yield: 2 servings

Vermicelli Casserole

2 tablespoons shortening
6 ounces uncooked
vermicelli, broken into
small pieces
1 pound ground beef
2 cloves garlic, minced
2 small onions, thinly
sliced
1 small bell pepper, thinly
sliced
4 ribs celery, thinly sliced
1 15-ounce can vacuum-
packed whole kernel
corn
2 teaspoons salt
½ teaspoon pepper
3 teaspoons chili powder
1 28-ounce can chopped
tomatoes
¾ cup water
8 ounces American cheese
slices

- Preheat oven to 300 degrees.
- Melt shortening in a large skillet. Sauté vermicelli until lightly browned, stirring occasionally. Add beef and cook until meat is browned.
- Stir in garlic, onion, bell pepper, celery, corn, salt, pepper, and chili powder. Add tomatoes and water. Cover and simmer for 25 minutes.
- Place in 9 by 13-inch baking dish; add cheese slices on top. Bake 20 minutes, or until cheese melts.

Yield: 8 servings

Note: Freezes well

Spaghetti and Meatballs

1 large onion, chopped
1 bell pepper, chopped
3 cloves garlic, minced
8 ounces fresh
  mushrooms, chopped
2 tablespoons olive oil
1 28-ounce can tomatoes
1 6-ounce can tomato
  paste
1 envelope spaghetti
  seasoning mix
2 cups chicken broth
1 tablespoon
  Worcestershire sauce
Hot cooked pasta

• Sauté onion, bell pepper, garlic, and mushrooms in olive oil. Add tomatoes, tomato paste, seasoning mix, broth, and Worcestershire sauce.

• Simmer slowly for 30 to 45 minutes. Add Meatballs; simmer to allow flavors to blend. Serve over pasta.

Note: This sauce is also good for seafood spaghetti. Add ¹/₂ pound shrimp and ¹/₂ pound scallops.

Meatballs

1 egg, beaten
2 slices white bread
2 pounds lean ground beef
2 tablespoons grated
  onion
1 teaspoon Italian
  seasoning

• To make Meatballs, mix egg and bread until bread falls apart. Add ground beef, onion, and seasoning. Blend well.

• Form mixture into meatballs. Broil until well done; drain.

Yield: 8 servings

Cheese Manicotti

8 ounces ground chuck
8 ounces ground sausage
1 clove garlic, minced
1 16-ounce can tomato
sauce
1 16-ounce can tomato
sauce with basil, garlic,
and onions
1 14-ounce can stewed
tomatoes with oregano,
onion, and green pepper
Salt
Pepper
½ cup seasoned bread
crumbs
15 ounces ricotta cheese
3 cups grated Cheddar
cheese, divided
3 cups grated mozzarella
cheese, divided
1 14-ounce package
manicotti

• Preheat oven to 350 degrees.
• Brown ground chuck and
sausage with garlic; drain.
Add tomato sauces, toma-
toes, and salt and pepper to
taste. Simmer while prepar-
ing cheese mixture.
• For cheese mixture, combine
bread crumbs, ricotta cheese,
2½ cups of the Cheddar
cheese, and 2½ cups of the
mozzarella cheese.
• Cook manicotti following
package directions. Stuff each
noodle with cheese mixture.
• Spread about ⅓ meat sauce
in 9 by 13-inch baking dish.
Place stuffed manicotti over
sauce, top with remaining
sauce; sprinkle with remaining cheese.
• Bake 35 minutes, or until
bubbly.

Yield: 8 to 10 servings

Note: Freezes well

175

Beef and Pork Lasagna

1 pound ground chuck
1 pound ground sausage
1 medium onion, finely
chopped
1 28-ounce can tomatoes,
drained
1 6-ounce can tomato
paste
1½ cups water
1 teaspoon garlic powder
½ teaspoon basil leaves
½ teaspoon oregano
Salt
Pepper
24 ounces cottage cheese
3 eggs
¾ cup Parmesan cheese
¼ cup parsley
1 8-ounce box lasagna
noodles
2 cups grated mozzarella
cheese

- Brown ground chuck, sausage, and onion; drain. Add tomatoes, tomato paste, water, garlic powder, basil, oregano, and salt and pepper to taste. Simmer 1 hour.
- Preheat oven to 350 degrees.
- In large bowl, combine cottage cheese, eggs, Parmesan cheese, and parsley.
- Cook lasagna noodles according to package directions.
- In a 9 by 13-inch baking dish, alternate layers of meat sauce, lasagna, and cottage cheese mixture. End with meat mixture. Top with mozzarella cheese.
- Bake 30 to 40 minutes.

Yield: 8 to 10 servings

Lasagna with Spinach

1 pound ground chuck
1 28-ounce can tomatoes
1 8-ounce can tomato
sauce
2 packages spaghetti sauce
mix
1 8-ounce package lasagna
noodles
1 10-ounce package frozen
chopped spinach
1 6-ounce package
mozzarella cheese,
grated
1 8-ounce carton cottage
cheese
½ cup Parmesan cheese

- Preheat oven to 350 degrees.
- Brown beef; drain. Add tomatoes, tomato sauce, and spaghetti sauce mix. Simmer 20 minutes.
- Cook lasagna noodles according to package directions.
- Cook spinach and drain.
- In a 9 by 13-inch baking dish, layer sauce, noodles, more sauce, mozzarella cheese, spinach, cottage cheese, more noodles, and sauce. Sprinkle Parmesan cheese over top.
- Bake 40 minutes, or until bubbly.

Yield: 8 servings

Italian Cheese-It Casserole

1½ pounds lean ground
beef
1 clove garlic, crushed
1 teaspoon salt
¼ teaspoon pepper
2 pounds zucchini, cooked
1 medium onion, chopped
1 4.5-ounce can chopped
green chilies
2 tablespoons butter,
melted
1 cup grated Cheddar
cheese
2 eggs, beaten
2 cups cottage cheese
2 teaspoons parsley
2 tablespoons Parmesan
cheese

- Preheat oven to 350 degrees.
- Mix ground beef, garlic, salt, and pepper in a skillet and cook until browned; drain. Spoon into a 9 by 13-inch baking dish.
- Mash zucchini; add onion, chilies, and butter. Layer over the beef mixture and sprinkle with Cheddar cheese.
- Combine eggs, cottage cheese, and parsley. Spoon over the zucchini layer. Sprinkle with Parmesan cheese.
- Bake 35 to 45 minutes.

Yield: 8 servings

Fabulous Fajitas

1½ pounds sirloin, cut into thin strips
2 tablespoons vegetable oil
2 tablespoons lemon juice
1 clove garlic, minced
1½ teaspoons ground cumin
1 teaspoon seasoned salt
½ teaspoon chili powder
¼ teaspoon crushed red pepper flakes
1 large bell pepper, thinly sliced
1 large onion, thinly sliced
8 7-inch flour tortillas
Grated Cheddar cheese
Salsa
Sour cream
Lettuce
Tomatoes

• In a skillet over medium heat, brown steak in oil. Place steak and drippings in a slow cooker. Add lemon juice, garlic, cumin, salt, chili powder, and red pepper flakes; mix well. Cover and cook on high for 2½ to 3 hours or until meat is tender.

• Add bell pepper and onion; cover and cook for 1 hour, or until vegetables are tender.

• Warm tortillas according to package directions; spoon beef and vegetables down the center of tortillas. Top each with cheese, salsa, sour cream, lettuce and tomatoes. Fold in sides of tortillas and serve immediately.

Yield: 4 servings

Mexican Enchiladas

1 pound ground chuck
1 clove garlic, minced
2 teaspoons salt
1 tablespoon chili powder
1 tablespoon water
1 cup kidney beans and
  juice
1 clove garlic, minced
½ medium onion, chopped
½ cup chopped bell
  pepper
3 tablespoons olive oil
1 28-ounce can Italian
  tomatoes
1 6-ounce can tomato
  paste
1 beef bouillon cube
¾ cup boiling water
3 tablespoons chopped
  chilies
Dash of cumin
½ teaspoon salt
⅛ teaspoon pepper
12 flour tortillas
1 cup grated Cheddar
  cheese

- Preheat oven to 350 degrees.
- Sauté ground chuck, garlic, salt, chili powder and 1 tablespoon water until meat is lightly browned. Pour off drippings. Add beans and mix.
- In a skillet, sauté garlic, onion, and bell pepper in olive oil until tender. Add tomatoes and tomato paste. Dissolve bouillon cube in ¾ cup hot water and add to tomato mixture. Add chilies, cumin, salt and pepper. Simmer 5 minutes.
- Put line of meat in center of flour tortilla and roll up. Place, seam side down, in greased 9 by 13-inch baking dish. Pour sauce over enchiladas. Spread cheese over top.
- Bake 25 to 30 minutes.

Yield: 6 servings

Reuben Casserole

1¾ cup sauerkraut,
drained
½ pound corned beef,
sliced
2 cups grated Swiss cheese
3 tablespoons Thousand
Island dressing
2 tomatoes, sliced
1 cup rye cracker crumbs
¼ pound (1 stick) butter
¼ teaspoon caraway seeds

• Preheat oven to 425 degrees.
• Layer sauerkraut, corned beef, and cheese in a 2-quart greased baking dish.
• Drizzle the dressing on top of the cheese. Place tomato slices on top of dressing.
• Sauté rye crumbs in butter; add caraway seeds. Sprinkle over top of casserole.
• Bake 30 minutes, or until heated through.

Yield: 4 servings

Lamb Shish Kabobs

3 1-pound lamb steaks
⅓ cup lemon juice
¼ cup olive oil
¼ cup finely chopped
onion
1 teaspoon salt
2 purple onions, quartered
24 snow pea pods
½ pound fresh mushrooms
1 15½-ounce can
pineapple chunks,
drained

• Trim fat from lamb; bone and cut into 1-inch cubes. Place in a large shallow dish.
• Combine lemon juice, oil, onion, and salt; pour over lamb. Cover and marinate in refrigerator 3 hours, turning occasionally. Drain, discarding marinade.
• Alternate lamb, purple onion, snow peas, mushrooms, and pineapple on 8 skewers. Grill, covered, over medium coals 5 minutes on each side or to desired degree of doneness.

Yield: 8 servings

Marinated Rack of Lamb

4 6-rib lamb rib roasts
1 cup Dale's marinade
1 cup dry white vermouth
3 tablespoons garlic
powder
2 tablespoons dry Italian
seasoning

• Place lamb in a shallow dish.

• Combine marinade, vermouth, garlic powder, and Italian seasoning. Pour 1 cup marinade mixture over lamb. Refrigerate lamb and reserved marinade mixture for 8 hours; turning lamb frequently.

• Remove meat from marinade. Place fat side up on a rack in a shallow roasting pan.

• Bake at 325 degrees for 1 hour and 15 minutes or until a meat thermometer registers 150 degrees, basting often with reserved marinade.

Yield: 12 servings

Orange-and-Ginger-Glazed Pork Roast

2 tablespoons chopped
fresh thyme or
2 teaspoons dried thyme
1 tablespoon chopped
fresh sage or 1 teaspoon
dried sage
2 teaspoons salt
1 teaspoon freshly ground
pepper
¼ teaspoon ground allspice
or cloves
2 cloves garlic, minced
2 tablespoons vegetable oil
1 3½ to 4 pound boneless
pork loin, tied for
roasting
½ cup (5 ounces) orange
marmalade
⅓ cup (3 ounces) Dijon
mustard
1 tablespoon grated fresh
ginger
1 tablespoon
Worcestershire sauce
¼ teaspoon salt (may use
up to ½ teaspoon)
¼ teaspoon freshly ground
pepper (may use up to
½ teaspoon)

- In a small bowl, combine thyme, sage, salt, pepper, allspice or cloves, and garlic to make a dry marinade.

- Rub oil over the pork; coat evenly with dry marinade. Let stand at least 1 hour, or cover and refrigerate several hours. Meanwhile, in a small bowl, stir together the remaining ingredients.

- Prepare a fire for indirect-heat cooking in a covered grill. Position the oiled grill rack 4 to 6 inches above the fire.

- Place the pork on the rack so it is not directly over the fire; cover the grill and open the vents halfway. Cook for 45 minutes; turn roast. Add more coals if necessary to maintain a constant temperature. Cook for 40 to 50 additional minutes, brushing with marmalade mixture every 10 minutes and turning roast once or twice. The pork is done when a meat thermometer registers 160 degrees.

- Remove from grill, cover loosely with aluminum foil; let rest for 10 minutes. To serve, snip the strings and cut into ¼-inch slices.

Yield: 8 servings

Pork Tenderloin

¼ cup soy sauce
2½ tablespoons red wine
1 tablespoon brown sugar
1 tablespoon honey
½ teaspoon cinnamon
1 clove garlic, crushed
1 green onion, chopped
2 whole pork tenderloins,
   fat removed

• To prepare marinade, combine soy sauce, wine, sugar, honey, cinnamon, garlic, and onion in a shallow dish. Add tenderloins, turning to coat evenly. Cover and let stand at room temperature 1 hour or refrigerate overnight, turning to keep coated.

• Preheat oven to 350 degrees.

• Drain and reserve juice. Bake 45 minutes, basting occasionally with juice. Cool and slice.

Yield: 6 to 8 servings

Pork Chops Creole

6 pork chops
Salt
Pepper
Flour
3 tablespoons vegetable oil
1 medium onion, chopped
2 tablespoons chopped bell
   pepper
1 28-ounce can tomatoes
1 tablespoon
   Worcestershire sauce
3 cups hot cooked rice

• Season pork chops with salt and pepper to taste; dredge in flour. Brown chops in oil until almost done. Drain and set aside.

• Sauté onion and bell pepper in oil used for chops. Add tomatoes and Worcestershire sauce; return pork chops to sauce.

• Simmer slowly until sauce is thick and meat is tender. Serve with hot rice.

Yield: 6 servings

Slow-Cooked Pork Ribs

¾ cup packed brown sugar
½ cup soy sauce
½ cup ketchup
¼ cup honey
2 tablespoons cider or
white wine vinegar
3 cloves garlic, minced
1 teaspoon ground ginger
1 teaspoon salt
¼ teaspoon crushed red
pepper flakes (may use
up to ½ teaspoon)
5 pounds country-style
pork ribs
1 medium onion, sliced
2 tablespoons sesame
seeds, toasted
2 tablespoons chopped
green onions

- In a large bowl, combine the brown sugar, soy sauce, ketchup, honey, vinegar, garlic, ginger, salt, and red pepper flakes. Add ribs and turn to coat.

- Place the onion in a 5-quart slow cooker; arrange ribs on top. Cover and cook on low for 5 to 6 hours or until a meat thermometer reads 160 to 170 degrees.

- Place ribs on a serving platter; sprinkle with sesame seeds and green onions.

Yield: 6 servings

185

Mustard-Glazed Baby Back Ribs

2 tablespoons vegetable
oil
1 small onion, chopped
1 cup honey
1 cup Dijon mustard
½ cup cider vinegar
½ teaspoon salt, plus salt
to taste
1 teaspoon ground cloves
6 pounds, more or less,
baby back ribs, in slabs
Freshly ground pepper

• Heat vegetable oil in a sauce-pan over moderate heat. Add onion and cook until soft, about 5 minutes. Add honey, mustard, vinegar, ½ teaspoon of the salt, and cloves. Stir well and bring to a boil. Reduce the heat and simmer for about 5 minutes, stirring occasionally. Remove from heat; set aside.

• Prepare a fire for indirect-heat cooking in a covered grill. Position the oiled grill rack 4 to 6 inches above the fire. Generously salt and pepper the ribs on both sides. Place ribs on rack, cover grill, and open vents halfway. Cook 40 minutes, turning once.

• Brush tops of ribs with honey mixture; cover and cook an additional 10 minutes. Turn ribs, brush with more sauce; cover and cook 10 minutes longer. (Total cooking time is approximately 1 hour.) Remove from grill; cut into single-rib pieces. Mound on a warmed platter and pass any remaining sauce at the table.

Yield: 4 to 6 servings

Pork Parmigiana

1 large egg
1 tablespoon water
2 tablespoons grated
Parmesan cheese
⅓ cup Italian-seasoned
bread crumbs
4 1¼-inch-thick slices
pork tenderloin
(about 8 ounces)
2 tablespoons vegetable oil
1 cup commercial spaghetti
sauce
½ cup (2 ounces) shredded
mozzarella cheese

- Preheat oven to 350 degrees.
- Combine egg and water;
  set aside.
- Combine Parmesan cheese
  and bread crumbs; set aside.
- Place each piece of pork
  between 2 sheets of heavy-
  duty plastic wrap; flatten to
  ¼-inch thickness, using a
  meat mallet or rolling pin.
  Dip pork in egg mixture, and
  dredge in crumb mixture.
- Cook pork slices in oil in a
  large skillet over medium heat
  just until browned, turning
  once. Arrange pork in a
  lightly greased 8-inch square
  baking dish; top with
  spaghetti sauce.
- Bake 25 minutes; top with
  mozzarella cheese. Bake
  5 additional minutes.

Yield: 4 servings

Herbed Pork Pinwheels

3 small sweet red bell
  peppers, chopped
¾ cup chopped onion
¾ cup chopped celery
1½ teaspoons dried thyme,
  crushed
¾ teaspoon garlic salt
¾ teaspoon ground red
  pepper
¾ teaspoon paprika
3 tablespoons vegetable oil
3 ¾-pound pork tenderloins
1½ tablespoons fennel
  seeds, crushed
1½ teaspoons lemon
  pepper

- Sauté red bell pepper, onion, celery, thyme, garlic salt, ground red pepper, and paprika in hot oil until vegetables are tender; set aside.
- Slice each pork tenderloin lengthwise down center, cutting to, but not through, the bottom. Place each between heavy-duty plastic or wax paper; pound to a 12 by 8-inch rectangle of even thickness using a meat mallet.
- Preheat oven to 325 degrees.
- Spoon ⅓ of pepper mixture onto tenderloin, spreading to within ½ inch of sides; roll tenderloin jelly-roll fashion, starting with short side. Tie with heavy string at 1½-inch intervals.
- Combine fennel seeds and lemon pepper; rub on top and sides of tenderloins. Place seam side down in shallow pan.
- Bake 45 minutes. Let stand 10 minutes; remove string and slice.

Yield: 8 to 10 servings

Smoked Sausage Dinner

⅓ cup vegetable oil
5 medium red potatoes,
  peeled and sliced
1 small head cabbage,
  sliced
1 medium onion, diced
1 1-pound package smoked
  sausage, sliced
Salt
Pepper

- Combine all ingredients in a Dutch oven. Cover and simmer over low heat until vegetables are tender, stirring occasionally.
- Remove lid; sauté until potatoes are light brown, about 30 minutes.

Yield: 4 to 6 servings

Note: Great served with cornbread.

Crock Pot Boston Butt Barbecue

1 Boston butt roast
Creole seasoning or salt
  and pepper
1 2-liter bottle cola-
  flavored soda
1 18-ounce bottle
  commercial barbecue
  sauce

- Sprinkle roast heavily with Creole seasoning or salt and pepper.
- Place roast in slow cooker; pour soda over roast. Cook all day or overnight until very tender.
- Preheat oven to 350 degrees.
- Pour off liquid in slow cooker; pull meat apart using 2 forks. Add barbecue sauce; bake, uncovered, in a 9 by 13-inch baking dish 30 minutes.

Yield: 8 to 10 servings

Sausage Dressing

1 pound ground sausage
1 large onion, chopped
2 stalks celery, chopped
½ cup butter
5 cups cornbread crumbs
1½ cups bread crumbs
   (about 3 slices)
1 tablespoon poultry
   seasoning
2 14½-ounce cans chicken
   broth, heated
1 teaspoon salt
¼ teaspoon pepper

• Preheat oven to 350 degrees.
• Brown sausage in a skillet; drain.
• Sauté onion and celery in butter.
• In a large bowl, combine bread crumbs, onion mixture, poultry seasoning, and sausage. Add broth and mix well. Season with salt and pepper. Spoon into a 9 by 13-inch baking dish.
• Bake 30 minutes.

Yield: 10 servings

Note: For a highly seasoned dressing, use hot ground sausage. Doubles or triples easily.

Deuce and a Quarter Pork Loin

Pork loin
Olive oil
Garlic powder
Lemon pepper

• Rub loin with olive oil, garlic powder, and lemon pepper.
• Smoke over 250 degree fire with apple and peach chips for 2¼ hours. If apple and peach chips are unavailable, hickory, mesquite, or wood of choice can be used.

Sauce

¼ pound (1 stick) butter
1 cup brown sugar
2 lemons, juiced
2 oranges, juiced
2 tablespoons grape jelly
¼ cup honey

• Melt butter in a saucepan over low heat. Add remaining ingredients. Baste meat 2 or 3 times while smoking. When done, slice meat and drizzle sauce on top.

Yield: 8 to 10 servings

Pork Cutlets in Caper Sauce

8 2½ to 3-ounce pork
  cutlets, flattened to
  ⅛ inch
Seasoned flour
3 large eggs, beaten
3 cups fresh white bread
  crumbs
¾ cup (1½ sticks) butter,
  divided
6 tablespoons olive oil,
  divided
1 clove garlic, minced
1½ cups chopped onion
  (about 2 onions)
8 anchovy fillets, scraped
  free of salt and minced
2 tablespoons balsamic
  vinegar
1 cup chicken broth
2 tablespoons capers
¼ cup Italian parsley,
  chopped
Black pepper

- Bread cutlets by dredging in seasoned flour, dipping into egg, and rolling in bread crumbs.

- In a large skillet, sauté cutlets in 4 tablespoons of the butter and 4 tablespoons of the olive oil until golden brown on both sides. Remove and drain well. Keep warm.

- Meanwhile, to make sauce, melt 4 tablespoons of the butter in a skillet over medium-high heat; add the remaining 2 tablespoons olive oil. Sauté garlic until aroma fills the air. Add onion and cook until lightly browned. Stir in anchovies; blend well.

- Mix in vinegar, broth, and capers, cooking until reduced. Swirl in remaining 4 tablespoons butter, parsley, and black pepper.

- Arrange hot cutlets on a serving platter, pouring sauce over all. Serve immediately.

Yield: 4 servings

Anthony Seta
Certified Master Chef
Memphis, Tennessee

Chicken Salad

8 cups diced cooked chicken
3 cups diced celery
4 slices crisp bacon,
crumbled
1 cup mayonnaise, more or
less
1 cup sour cream
2 tablespoons lemon juice
3 tablespoons sweet pickle
juice
5 hard-boiled eggs, chopped
Salt
Pepper

- In a large mixing bowl, combine all ingredients, mixing well.
- Refrigerate until flavors are blended.

Yield: 8 servings

Exotic Chicken Salad

8 cups cubed cooked
chicken breasts
2 8-ounce cans sliced
water chestnuts, drained
2 cups chopped celery
2 pounds fresh seedless
white grapes, whole
3 cups toasted sliced
almonds, divided
2 cups mayonnaise
1 teaspoon curry powder
2 tablespoons soy sauce
2 tablespoons lemon juice
1 20-ounce can chunk
pineapple, drained,
divided
Lettuce leaves

- Combine chicken, water chestnuts, celery, grapes, and 1½ cups of the almonds in a large mixing bowl.
- In a separate smaller bowl, mix the mayonnaise, curry powder, soy sauce, lemon juice, and pineapple, reserving 1 cup pineapple for garnish.
- Spoon mayonnaise mixture over chicken; gently stir until well-mixed. Chill for several hours. Serve on lettuce leaves and garnish with remaining almonds and pineapple chunks.

Yield: 12 servings

Fruited Chicken Salad (for Forty)

2 20-ounce cans pineapple
chunks
20 cups cubed cooked
chicken
12 cups cooked rice
8 cups seedless green
grape halves
4 cups sliced celery
4 15-ounce cans mandarin
oranges, drained
4 8-ounce cans sliced
water chestnuts, drained
and halved
4 cups mayonnaise or
salad dressing
7 tablespoons frozen
orange juice concentrate
1 to 2 tablespoons salt
1 teaspoon pepper
4 cups slivered almonds,
lightly toasted

• Drain the pineapple, reserving 2 tablespoons juice.
Combine pineapple chunks,
chicken, rice, grape halves,
celery, oranges, and water
chestnuts. Set aside.

• In a separate bowl, mix the
mayonnaise, concentrate,
salt, pepper, and reserved
pineapple juice until smooth;
gently toss with chicken
mixture. Chill several hours
or overnight.

• Garnish with almonds just
before serving.

Yield: 40 to 50 servings

Chicken Salad with Caesar Dressing

1 large head romaine
  lettuce
12 ounces small red
  potatoes, halved
¼ cup fresh lemon juice
2 anchovy fillets, drained
  and blotted dry, chopped
1 tablespoon red wine
  vinegar
1 clove garlic, minced
⅓ cup extra-virgin olive oil
3 cups cooked chicken, cut
  into wide strips (4 half
  breasts or 1 whole
  chicken)
12 diagonal slices (¼-inch)
  peeled cucumber
¼ cup freshly grated
  Parmesan cheese,
  divided
12 cherry tomatoes,
  halved, for garnish
Freshly ground black
  pepper
½ cup sliced almonds,
  toasted until golden in
  dry skillet, optional

- Wash, trim, and tear lettuce into bite-size pieces. Wrap in kitchen towel; keep crisp in refrigerator until ready to use.
- Place potatoes in saucepan; cover with water. Bring to a boil. Cook, covered, until potatoes are tender, about 15 minutes. Drain and set aside.
- Combine lemon juice, anchovies, vinegar, and garlic in blender or food processor. With motor running, gradually add olive oil until dressing is blended.
- Place chicken in medium bowl and toss with half of the dressing.
- In separate large bowl, toss lettuce, cooked potatoes, cucumber slices, and 2 tablespoons of the Parmesan cheese with the remaining dressing. Divide salad evenly among 4 large dinner plates. Top with chicken, dividing evenly. Sprinkle with remaining 2 tablespoons Parmesan cheese. Garnish plates with tomatoes. Add grinding of black pepper to each salad. Sprinkle with toasted almonds.

Yield: 4 servings

Chicken Crescent Delights

6 ounces cream cheese, softened
¼ pound (1 stick) butter, divided
4 cups chopped cooked chicken
¼ cup milk
½ teaspoon salt
2 tablespoons chopped onion
2 tablespoons chopped pimiento
2 8-ounce cans refrigerated crescent rolls
¾ cup crumbled seasoned croutons

• Preheat oven to 350 degrees.
• In a medium bowl, blend cream cheese and 5 table-spoons of the butter. Add the chicken, milk, salt, onion, and pimiento. Mix well.
• Separate dough into 8 rectangles. Press perfora-tions to seal. Spoon ½ cup of chicken mixture into center of rectangle. Pull four corners of dough to top center of filling. Twist firmly and press out any perfora-tions. Place on baking sheet; drizzle with remaining butter and crumbled croutons.
• Bake 30 minutes, or until golden brown.

Yield: 8 servings

Spicy Baked Chicken

1 4-pound fryer, whole
1½ teaspoons salt
½ teaspoon ground red pepper
1 teaspoon black pepper
1 teaspoon cinnamon
1 teaspoon allspice

• Preheat oven to 325 degrees.
• Clean chicken and season well inside and out, with salt, peppers, cinnamon, and allspice. Bake, uncovered, 2½ to 3 hours, basting occasionally with pan juices.

Yield: 4 servings

Hawaiian Chicken

4 chicken breasts
½ cup all-purpose flour
⅓ cup vegetable oil
1 teaspoon salt
¼ teaspoon pepper
1 20-ounce can sliced
pineapple
1 cup sugar
2 tablespoons cornstarch
¾ cup cider vinegar
1 tablespoon soy sauce
¼ teaspoon ginger
1 chicken bouillon cube
1 large bell pepper, cut
crosswise into ¼-inch-
thick circles
Hot cooked rice

- Wash chicken; pat dry with paper towels. Coat chicken with flour.

- Heat oil in a large skillet. Add chicken, a few pieces at a time; brown on all sides. Remove to shallow roasting pan, arranging pieces skin side up. Sprinkle with salt and pepper.

- Preheat oven to 350 degrees.

- To make sauce, drain pineapple, pouring juice into a 2-cup measure. Add water to make 1¼ cups. In a medium saucepan, combine sugar, cornstarch, pineapple juice, vinegar, soy sauce, ginger, and bouillon cube; bring to a boil, stirring constantly. Boil 2 minutes. Pour over chicken.

- Bake, uncovered, 30 minutes. Add pineapple slices and bell pepper; bake 30 additional minutes, or until chicken is tender. Serve with rice.

Yield: 4 servings

Lemon Chicken

2 lemons
4 boneless, skinless
    chicken breast halves
¼ cup all-purpose flour
½ teaspoon paprika
2 tablespoons vegetable oil
2 tablespoons brown sugar
1½ teaspoons salt
½ cup chicken broth

- Grate rind of 1 lemon. Set rind aside.
- Cut the same lemon in half; squeeze juice over chicken breasts.
- Combine flour and paprika; dredge chicken in seasoned flour.
- In a large skillet, heat oil and brown chicken on both sides. Sprinkle chicken with lemon rind, brown sugar, and salt. Add broth to skillet and bring to a simmer. Reduce heat to low, cover, and cook for 25 minutes.
- Slice remaining lemon; arrange over chicken. Cover and cook until chicken is tender and no longer pink.

Yield: 4 servings

Lemon Pepper Chicken

**6 boneless, skinless
  chicken breasts**
Lemon pepper
Lemon juice
Worcestershire sauce
¼ pound (1 stick) butter
**1 bunch green onions,
  chopped**
**½ pound fresh mushrooms,
  sliced**
**1 8-ounce carton whipping
  cream**

- In a shallow glass dish, marinate chicken breasts in lemon pepper, lemon juice, and Worcestershire sauce for 1 hour. Remove chicken and drain, discarding marinade.

- In a large skillet, melt butter; sauté marinated breasts 10 minutes on each side, or until browned. Remove and keep warm.

- In the same skillet, sauté green onions and mushrooms until tender. Pour in whipping cream and simmer until heated through. Serve sauce over warm breasts.

Yield: 6 servings

Stir-Fried Chicken

2 tablespoons vegetable oil
2 cups uncooked chicken,
   cubed
½ cup sliced green onions,
   including tops
⅔ cup diagonally sliced
   celery
1½ cups sliced bell pepper
1 8-ounce can sliced water
   chestnuts
1 10-ounce package frozen
   snow peas
1 8¾-ounce can pineapple
   chunks or tidbits and
   juice
¼ cup chicken broth
¼ cup brown sugar
1 tablespoon cornstarch
½ teaspoon ground ginger
2 tablespoons vinegar
2 tablespoons soy sauce
½ teaspoon salt
¼ teaspoon pepper
Hot cooked rice or noodles

- In a wok or large skillet, heat oil; add chicken. Stir over high heat 5 minutes. Add onions, celery, bell pepper, and water chestnuts; continue cooking 2 minutes.

- Stir in snow peas, pineapple and juice, and broth. Stir-fry 2 additional minutes.

- In a separate bowl, mix sugar, cornstarch, ginger, vinegar, soy sauce, salt, and pepper. Pour over stir-fry. Reduce heat and simmer until thickened. Do not overcook.

- Serve over rice or noodles.

Yield: 8 servings

Cajun Chicken

**2 pounds chicken, cut into
serving pieces**
1 quart buttermilk
1 tablespoon seasoned salt
**4 tablespoons Cajun
seasoning**

• Place chicken in a zip-top
plastic bag.

• In a mixing bowl, combine
buttermilk, seasoned salt, and
Cajun seasoning; whisk
together well.

• Pour buttermilk mixture into
bag over chicken. Close bag
and place in a large bowl.
Refrigerate overnight.

• Preheat oven to 325 degrees.

• Drain chicken; place in a
large greased casserole dish.
Bake 1½ hours, or until
tender.

Yield: 4 servings

Lemon, Garlic, and Rosemary Chicken

2 garlic bulbs, minced
1 cup fresh lemon juice
1½ teaspoons freshly
ground pepper
1 tablespoon salt
⅔ cup fresh rosemary
sprigs, coarsely chopped
2 cups olive oil
3 2½-to-3-pound whole
chickens, cut up
3 lemons, sliced
Fresh rosemary sprigs for
garnish

• Whisk together garlic, lemon juice, pepper, salt, and rosemary until blended; whisk in oil. Pour mixture evenly into three large heavy-duty, zip-top plastic bags; add chicken pieces and lemon slices. Seal and chill 8 hours, turning bags occasionally.

• Preheat oven to 425 degrees.

• Line two 10 by 15-inch jelly-roll pans with heavy-duty aluminum foil. Remove chicken from marinade, reserving marinade. Arrange chicken in pans. Drizzle with marinade.

• Bake, uncovered, 1 hour, or until done, basting with pan juices every 20 minutes. Garnish, if desired.

Yield: 12 servings

Chicken Strips with Plum Sauce

**6 to 8 boneless, skinless
chicken breasts
1½ cups buttermilk
2 teaspoons lemon juice
2 teaspoons
Worcestershire sauce
1 teaspoon soy sauce
1 teaspoon paprika
1 tablespoon Greek
Seasoning
1 teaspoon salt
1 teaspoon pepper
2 cloves garlic, minced or
¼ teaspoon garlic
powder
4 cups soft bread crumbs
½ cup sesame seeds
4 to 8 tablespoons butter,
melted**

- Cut chicken into ½-inch strips. Combine buttermilk, lemon juice, Worcestershire sauce, soy sauce, paprika, Greek seasoning, salt, pepper, and garlic in a shallow dish. Add chicken, mixing until well coated. Cover; refrigerate for several hours.
- Preheat oven to 350 degrees.
- Combine bread crumbs and sesame seeds, mixing well. Drain chicken thoroughly, discarding marinade. Add chicken to crumb mixture; toss to coat.
- Place chicken in a greased 9 by 13-inch baking dish (may take 2 dishes). Brush with melted butter.
- Bake 35 to 40 minutes. Serve with Plum Sauce.

Yield: 6 to 8 servings

Plum Sauce

**1½ cups red plum jam
1½ tablespoons prepared
mustard
1½ tablespoons prepared
horseradish
1½ teaspoons lemon juice**

- Combine jam, mustard, horseradish, and lemon juice in a small saucepan, mixing well. Place over low heat just until warm, stirring constantly.

Yield: 1¾ cups

Pecan Chicken Fingers

6 boneless, skinless
chicken breast halves
1 cup all-purpose flour
1 cup pecans, toasted and
ground
¼ cup sesame seeds
1 tablespoon paprika
¾ teaspoon salt
⅛ teaspoon pepper
1 large egg, lightly beaten
1 cup buttermilk
⅓ cup butter, melted
Lettuce and lemon slices
for garnish

- Preheat oven to 375 degrees.
- Cut each chicken breast half into 4 strips. Combine flour, pecans, sesame seeds, paprika, salt, and pepper; set aside.
- Combine egg and buttermilk. Dip chicken strips into buttermilk mixture, and dredge in flour mixture.
- Pour butter into a 10 by 15-inch jelly-roll pan; add chicken, turning to coat. Bake 30 minutes; drain. Garnish, if desired.

Yield: 4 to 6 servings

Golden Chicken Nuggets

½ cup dry bread crumbs
¼ cup grated Parmesan
cheese
2 teaspoons Italian
seasoning
1 teaspoon salt
6 boneless, skinless
chicken breast halves,
cut into 1-inch cubes
½ cup butter, melted

- Preheat oven to 400 degrees.
- Combine bread crumbs, Parmesan cheese, seasoning, and salt in a shallow dish. Dip chicken cubes in butter; roll in crumb mixture.
- Place in a single layer on an ungreased 10 by 15-inch baking pan. Bake 12 to 15 minutes, or until juices run clear.

Yield: 4 dozen

Overnight Chicken

2 cups sour cream
¼ cup lemon juice
4 teaspoons
  Worcestershire sauce
3 teaspoons salt
4 teaspoons celery salt
2 teaspoons paprika
1 teaspoon garlic salt
½ teaspoon pepper
8 boneless, skinless
  chicken breasts
Cracker crumbs, using a
  combination of saltines,
  wheat, and sesame
  crackers
Butter, melted

- In a shallow glass dish, combine the sour cream, lemon juice, Worcestershire sauce, salt, celery salt, paprika, garlic salt, and pepper. Marinate chicken breasts in this mixture overnight.
- Preheat oven to 325 degrees.
- Drain breasts, discarding marinade; roll chicken in cracker crumbs. Bake 30 minutes. Drizzle with butter; bake an additional 30 minutes, or until tender and golden.

Yield: 8 servings

Crunchy Parmesan Chicken

1 2.8-ounce can French-
  fried onions, crushed
¾ cup grated Parmesan
  cheese
¼ cup dry bread crumbs
1 teaspoon paprika
½ teaspoon salt
Dash of pepper
1 egg, beaten
1 tablespoon milk
1 2½ to 3-pound broiler-
  fryer chicken, cut up
¼ cup butter, melted

- Preheat oven to 350 degrees.
- Combine onion, cheese, bread crumbs, paprika, salt, and pepper, mixing well. Combine egg and milk.
- Dip chicken pieces in egg mixture, and coat well with crumb mixture. Place in a greased 9 by 13-inch baking dish; spoon butter over chicken.
- Bake 1 hour, or until golden brown.

Yield: 4 servings

Teriyaki Chicken

¾ cup chopped onion
2 cloves garlic, minced
Pinch of ground ginger
2½ tablespoons sugar
½ cup soy sauce
1 cup water
6 boneless, skinless
　chicken breast halves
6 slices pineapple
6 slices mozzarella cheese

- Combine onion, garlic, ginger, sugar, soy sauce, and water in a shallow glass dish. Add chicken, turning to coat evenly. Marinate 12 to 14 hours.
- Drain chicken, discarding marinade. Grill over medium coals 25 minutes, or until juices run clear.
- Top each piece with slice of pineapple and slice of cheese. Broil until cheese is melted.

Yield: 6 servings

Grilled Tarragon Chicken

2 teaspoons Dijon mustard
4 boneless, skinless
　chicken breast halves
¼ teaspoon pepper
⅓ cup butter, melted
2 teaspoons lemon juice
2 teaspoons minced fresh
　tarragon or ½ teaspoon
　dried tarragon
½ teaspoon garlic salt

- Spread mustard on both sides of chicken; sprinkle with pepper. Cover and refrigerate at least 2 hours.
- Combine remaining ingredients, mixing well.
- Grill over hot coals until juices run clear, basting with butter mixture during last 3 to 5 minutes.

Yield: 4 servings

205

Grilled Lemon Chicken

**20 chicken drumsticks
(about 3 pounds) or
chicken pieces of choice
1½ cups vegetable oil
1 cup lemon juice
1½ tablespoons onion
powder
1½ tablespoons dried basil
1 tablespoon salt
2 teaspoons paprika
1 teaspoon dried thyme
2 cloves garlic, pressed**

• Place chicken in a heavy-duty, zip-top plastic bag; set aside.

• Combine the remaining ingredients in a jar. Cover and shake vigorously. Pour 2 cups over chicken; refrigerate remaining ½ cup mixture. Seal bag, and refrigerate 4 hours, turning occasionally.

• Remove drumsticks from marinade, discarding marinade. Cook, covered with grill lid, over medium coals (300 to 350 degrees) 20 minutes on each side, basting occasionally with the reserved ½ cup marinade.

Yield: 8 to 10 servings

Chicken Kabobs

**2 teaspoons ground
mustard**
**1 tablespoon
Worcestershire sauce**
½ cup water
½ cup soy sauce
1 tablespoon vegetable oil
**4 boneless, skinless
chicken breast halves**
**2 medium zucchini, cut into
1½-inch slices**
**1 medium onion, cut into
wedges**
**1 medium bell pepper, cut
into chunks**
**8 to 12 medium fresh
mushrooms**

- In a zip-top plastic bag, combine the mustard and Worcestershire sauce. Add the water, soy sauce, and oil; remove ⅓ cup and set aside for basting.

- Cut chicken into 1½-inch pieces; add to bag. Seal and refrigerate 1½ to 2 hours. Drain, discarding marinade.

- Thread chicken and vegetables alternately on skewers. Baste with reserved marinade.

- Grill over hot coals 10 minutes. Turn and baste. Cook 10 additional minutes, or until chicken juices run clear.

Yield: 4 to 6 servings

Beer-Roasted Chicken

1 3 to 4-pound chicken, whole
1 12-ounce can beer, divided (see Basting Sauce)
Butter spray
Lemon pepper seasoning

- Wash chicken; place on beer can, which contains 6 ounces of beer (reserving other 6 ounces for Basting Sauce). Wings of chicken should be at the top of the can with the legs at the bottom. Secure wings to the chicken with wooden picks.
- Spray chicken lightly with butter spray. Sprinkle entire chicken with lemon pepper to taste.
- Place can with chicken on grill grate over medium coals. Cook 2 hours, or until golden brown, basting every 15 to 20 minutes with the following Sauce:

Sauce

2 cups Basting Sauce*
¼ teaspoon garlic powder
6 ounces beer
2 tablespoons commercially-prepared dry rub

- Combine all ingredients, mixing well.

*Refer to Basting Sauce on page 261 in Sauce Section.

Yield: 4 servings

Festive Chicken and Artichokes

4 tablespoons butter
4 tablespoons all-purpose
flour
2½ cups milk or cream
2 cups grated Swiss
cheese, divided
2 cups grated Cheddar
cheese, divided
4 8½-ounce cans artichoke
hearts, drained
1 10¾-ounce can cream of
mushroom soup
1 10¾-ounce can cream of
celery soup
16 ounces sour cream
4 tablespoons sherry
1 teaspoon salt
1 teaspoon black pepper
½ teaspoon
Worcestershire sauce
¼ teaspoon hot sauce
10 cups cooked chicken
breasts, cut into bite-
size pieces
4 4-ounce cans button
mushrooms, drained
Freshly grated Parmesan
cheese
Paprika

- Preheat oven to 350 degrees.
- To make cream sauce, melt butter in a saucepan; slowly add flour, mixing well. Pour in milk slowly, whisking until smooth. Cook over medium heat, stirring constantly, until thickened. Add 1 cup of the Swiss cheese and 1 cup of the Cheddar cheese, stirring until cheese is melted.
- Slice each artichoke into 2 or 3 pieces. Set aside.
- In a mixing bowl, combine cream sauce, soups, sour cream, sherry, salt, pepper, Worcestershire sauce, and hot sauce.
- Layer chicken, artichokes, and mushrooms in 2 greased 9 by 13-inch baking dishes; pour in sauce. Sprinkle with the remaining 1 cup Swiss cheese, the remaining 1 cup Cheddar cheese, the Parmesan cheese, and paprika.
- Bake 40 minutes, or until bubbly.

Yield: 15 to 20 servings

Crispy Chicken with Asparagus Sauce

**4 boneless, skinless
chicken breast halves
Salt
Pepper
1 egg or 2 egg whites,
beaten
½ cup dry bread crumbs
2 tablespoons vegetable oil
1 10¾-ounce can cream of
asparagus soup
⅓ cup milk
⅓ cup water
Hot cooked rice**

- Season chicken with salt and pepper to taste. Dip chicken in egg; coat evenly with bread crumbs.

- In hot oil, sauté chicken 15 minutes over medium heat, or until browned on both sides and no longer pink. Remove and drain well. Keep warm.

- In same skillet, combine soup, milk, and water over low heat. Heat thoroughly, stirring occasionally.

- Spoon soup mixture over chicken breasts. Serve with rice.

Yield: 4 servings

Chicken and Asparagus Casserole

12 boneless, skinless
chicken breast halves
1 medium onion, chopped
½ cup butter
1 8-ounce can sliced
mushrooms
1 10¾-ounce can cream of
chicken soup
1 10¾-ounce can cream of
mushroom soup
1 5½-ounce can
evaporated milk
½ pound sharp Cheddar
cheese, grated
¼ teaspoon Tabasco
2 teaspoons soy sauce
1 teaspoon salt
½ teaspoon black pepper
1 teaspoon Accent
1 2-ounce jar chopped
pimiento
2 14½-ounce cans whole
asparagus, drained
½ cup slivered almonds,
lightly toasted

• Cook chicken in small
amount of seasoned water
until tender; drain and cool.
Cut into bite-size pieces.
Set aside.

• Preheat oven to 350 degrees.

• Sauté onion in butter in a
Dutch oven or large skillet
until tender; add remaining
ingredients except asparagus
and almonds. Simmer until
cheese melts.

• To assemble, place a layer of
chicken in a greased 9 by
13-inch baking dish. Layer
with asparagus; add a layer of
sauce. Repeat layers, ending
with sauce. Sprinkle with
almonds on top.

• Bake 30 minutes, or until
bubbly.

Yield: 12 servings

Mozzarella Chicken

**6 boneless, skinless
chicken breasts
Seasoned salt
Black pepper
Parsley
1 large eggplant, diced
1 small onion, finely
chopped
1 chicken bouillon cube
dissolved in ½ cup
boiling water
½ cup Italian bread crumbs
½ cup plus 2 tablespoons
Parmesan cheese,
divided
8 slices mozzarella cheese,
divided
1 15-ounce can traditional-
style spaghetti sauce
Hot cooked pasta**

- Preheat oven to 400 degrees.
- Pound chicken breasts with a mallet until thinned; season with seasoned salt, pepper, and parsley. Set aside.
- In a skillet, sauté eggplant and onion in broth made from bouillon cube and water until very tender.
- Combine bread crumbs, ½ cup of the Parmesan cheese, and 1½ cups of eggplant mixture, blending well.
- Cut 2 cheese slices into 6 strips. Place cheese strips on chicken breasts. Spoon 1 tablespoon eggplant-bread crumb mixture on each breast; roll up and secure with wooden picks. Place breasts in a greased 9 by 13-inch baking dish. Bake 25 minutes.
- Meanwhile, combine the remaining 2 tablespoons Parmesan cheese, the remaining eggplant mixture, and spaghetti sauce in a saucepan. Bring to a boil and simmer 20 minutes.
- After 25 minutes, remove chicken from oven; drain excess juices and cover with spaghetti sauce mixture. Place remaining 6 mozzarella cheese slices on breasts. Bake, covered, for an additional 20 minutes. Serve with pasta.

Yield: 6 servings

Note: Fat-free Parmesan cheese and fat-free mozzarella cheese slices may be used to create a low-fat dinner.

Chick'n'Chiladas

1 cup chopped onion
⅓ cup chopped bell pepper
2 tablespoons vegetable oil
2 cups cooked chopped chicken
1½ cups grated colby and Monterey Jack cheese, divided
1 4-ounce can chopped green chilies
2 10¾-ounce cans cream of chicken soup
2 cups sour cream
½ teaspoon ground coriander
¼ teaspoon ground cumin
½ teaspoon salt, optional
6 8-inch flour tortillas

- Preheat oven to 350 degrees.
- In a large skillet, combine onion, bell pepper, and oil. Sauté over medium heat, stirring occasionally, 5 minutes or until vegetables are tender. Remove from heat. Add chicken, ½ cup of the cheese, and chilies to vegetable mixture. Set aside.
- To make sauce, combine soup, sour cream, coriander, cumin, and salt, if desired, in a medium saucepan. Simmer over low heat just until warm, stirring frequently. Do not boil. Stir ½ cup sauce into reserved chicken mixture.
- Warm tortillas according to package directions. Divide chicken mixture among tortillas. Roll up tortillas and place seam side down in a greased 9 by 13-inch baking dish. Pour remaining sauce over tortillas; sprinkle with remaining 1 cup cheese.
- Bake 25 to 30 minutes, or until cheese is melted and sauce is bubbly.

Yield: 6 servings

Chicken Lasagna

1 10-ounce package
frozen chopped spinach,
thawed and drained
2 cups (3 to 4 breasts)
chicken, cooked and
chopped
2 cups grated Cheddar
cheese
⅓ cup finely chopped
onion
1 tablespoon soy sauce
1 10¾-ounce can cream of
mushroom soup
1 8-ounce carton sour
cream
⅓ cup mayonnaise
Salt
Pepper
6 lasagna noodles, cooked
1 cup Parmesan cheese

- Preheat oven to 350 degrees.
- Combine spinach, chicken, cheese, onion, soy sauce, soup, sour cream, and mayonnaise, mixing gently but blending well. Season with salt and pepper to taste.
- In a greased 9 by 13-inch baking dish, layer lasagna and spinach-chicken mixture; repeat until all is used. Sprinkle with Parmesan cheese.
- To make Topping, melt butter in small skillet; sauté pecans 3 to 4 minutes, stirring constantly. Salt to taste. Cover casserole with topping.
- Bake, covered, 1 hour. Let stand 10 minutes before serving.

Topping

2 tablespoons butter
1 cup broken pecans
Salt

Yield: 8 to 10 servings

Note: This dish freezes well.

Country Chicken Pie

6 chicken breasts, cooked
and diced
1 10¾-ounce can cream of
mushroom soup
1 10¾-ounce can chicken
broth
½ cup plus 1 tablespoon
sour cream, divided
1 8½-ounce can English
peas, drained
1 4-ounce can chopped
mushrooms, drained
3 hard-boiled eggs, sliced
1 cup self-rising flour
1 cup milk
¼ pound (1 stick) butter,
melted
1 tablespoon sugar

- Preheat oven to 375 degrees.
- Place chicken in a greased
  8 by 8-inch baking dish.
  Combine soup, broth, and
  ½ cup of the sour cream.
  Pour over chicken. Layer
  peas, mushrooms, and eggs
  over sauce.
- In separate bowl, combine
  flour, milk, butter, the
  remaining 1 tablespoon
  sour cream, and sugar.
  Pour evenly over chicken
  and vegetables. Do not stir.
- Bake, uncovered, 1 hour,
  or until bubbly and golden
  brown.

Yield: 6 servings

Chicken and Dumplings

1 3 to 4-pound broiler-
  fryer chicken
2 quarts water
1 cup all-purpose flour
1 teaspoon salt
2 tablespoons shortening
1 egg, beaten
½ cup milk

• In a large Dutch oven or
  stock pot, boil chicken in
  water until tender. Remove
  chicken, reserving broth and
  keeping hot. Bone and cut
  chicken into chunks;
  set aside.

• Sift flour and salt into a
  mixing bowl; cut in shortening with a pastry blender or
  two knives until mixture
  resembles fine crumbs.
  Add egg and milk, working
  together but handling gently.

• Roll dough on floured board.
  Cut into 1-inch strips. Drop
  into hot broth. Gently stir in
  reserved chicken chunks.
  Cover and cook 20 to
  25 minutes.

Yield: 6 servings

Cornbread Dressing for Baked Chicken

2½ cups chopped celery
8 cups crumbled cornbread
2 cups bread crumbs
2½ cups chopped onion
¼ pound (1 stick) butter, melted
4 eggs, beaten (may use more if desired)
2 10¾-ounce cans cream of chicken soup
3½ cups chicken broth
1¼ teaspoons poultry seasoning
Salt
Pepper

- Preheat oven to 350 degrees.
- Combine all ingredients, mixing thoroughly. Spoon into a greased 9 by 13-inch baking dish.
- Bake 45 minutes, or until set.

Yield: 8 to 10 servings

Jalapeño-Glazed Cornish Hens

3 1½-pound Cornish hens, split
½ teaspoon salt
¼ teaspoon pepper
1 10½-ounce jar jalapeño jelly
2 teaspoons grated lime rind
⅓ cup lime juice
¼ cup vegetable oil
1 tablespoon chopped fresh cilantro

• Sprinkle hens with salt and pepper, and place, cut side down, in a large shallow dish; set aside.

• Melt jelly in a small saucepan over low heat; add lime rind and remaining ingredients. Pour jalapeño marinade over hens; cover and refrigerate 3 hours, turning occasionally.

• For a charcoal grill, prepare fire, and let burn until coals are white. Rake coals to opposite sides of grill; place a drip pan between coals and rack. For a gas grill, light one burner, placing drip pan on opposite side.

• Drain hens, reserving jalapeño marinade. Arrange hens on food rack over drip pan. Cook, covered with grill lid, over medium-hot coals (350 to 400 degrees) 35 minutes. Brush with jalapeño marinade; cook an additional 40 minutes.

Yield: 6 servings

Venison Tortillas

1 pound lean ground
  venison, crumbled
2 medium onions, chopped
  (2 cups)
3 medium tomatoes,
  chopped (3 cups)
¼ cup water
1 to 3 jalapeño peppers,
  seeded and sliced
1½ teaspoons ground
  cumin
1 teaspoon chili powder
½ teaspoon garlic powder
½ teaspoon salt
½ teaspoon freshly ground
  black pepper
¼ teaspoon red pepper
1 16-ounce can refried
  beans
8 flour tortillas
2 cups (8 ounces) grated
  Cheddar cheese
Salsa and sour cream for
  garnish

- In a 12-inch nonstick skillet, combine venison and onions. Cook over medium heat for six to eight minutes, or until meat is no longer pink, stirring occasionally. Drain.

- Stir in tomatoes, water, jalapeños, cumin, chili powder, garlic powder, salt, black pepper, and red pepper. Bring to a boil. Simmer for 30 to 40 minutes, or until liquid cooks away but mixture is still moist, stirring occasionally.

- In one-quart saucepan, heat beans over medium-low heat, stirring occasionally. Warm tortillas.

- Spoon ½ cup meat mixture and two heaping tablespoons of beans across the center of each tortilla. Sprinkle ¼ cup of cheese over each. Roll up tortilla, securing with wooden toothpick. If desired, heat until cheese is melted. Top with salsa and sour cream.

Yield: 8 tortillas

Mock Chicken-Fried Steak

1½ pounds lean ground venison, crumbled
⅓ cup finely chopped onion
¾ tablespoon seasoned salt
1½ cups butter-flavored cracker crumbs (36 crackers)
1 egg, beaten
¼ cup skim milk
3 tablespoons vegetable oil, divided

• In a large mixing bowl, combine venison, onion, and salt. Shape mixture into six half-inch-thick patties.

• Place crumbs in a shallow dish. In a second shallow dish, combine egg and milk.

• Dip patties first in egg mixture, then dredge in crumbs to coat. Heat 1½ tablespoons of the oil in 12-inch nonstick skillet over medium heat. Cook three patties for 4 to 6 minutes, or until browned and meat is no longer pink inside, turning patties over once.

• Remove patties from skillet. Set aside and keep warm. Repeat with remaining oil and patties.

Yield: 6 servings

Grilled Venison Roast

8½ pound bone-in venison
  roast, trimmed
2 cloves garlic, halved
½ cup Worcestershire
  sauce
2 tablespoons soy sauce
2 teaspoons garlic powder
2 teaspoons lemon-pepper
  seasoning
Hickory chips

Sauce

4 14½-ounce cans chicken
  broth
1 10-ounce jar red currant
  jelly
½ cup bourbon
1 tablespoon gin
2 tablespoons black
  peppercorns
¼ teaspoon dried thyme
2 tablespoons reserved pan
  drippings

• Place venison in a roasting
  pan. Cut 4 slits in venison,
  and insert garlic halves.
  Combine Worcestershire
  sauce and soy sauce, and
  pour over venison; sprinkle all
  sides with garlic powder and
  lemon-pepper seasoning.
  Cover and refrigerate 2 hours.

• Soak hickory chips in water
  30 minutes. Prepare charcoal fire on sides of grill
  around a drip pan; let burn
  30 minutes. Place venison
  on grill rack over pan. Cook,
  covered with grill lid, over
  low coals (250 degrees)
  3 hours or until meat thermometer inserted in thickest
  portion of meat registers
  140 degrees or desired
  degree of doneness. Carefully remove drip pan, and
  reserve 2 tablespoons
  drippings to use in Sauce.

• To prepare Sauce, combine
  chicken broth, jelly, bourbon,
  gin, peppercorns, and thyme
  in a saucepan; bring to a boil
  over high heat. Reduce heat,
  and simmer about 1 hour or
  until liquid is reduced to 4
  cups. Pour mixture through a
  large wire-mesh strainer into
  a 4-cup liquid measuring cup,
  discarding peppercorns. Stir
  in 2 tablespoons reserved
  pan drippings. Serve Sauce
  with warm venison.

Yield: 12 servings

Venison Parmesan

1 large onion, chopped
½ cup plus 3 tablespoons
vegetable oil, divided
1 6-ounce can tomato
paste
1 clove garlic, crushed
2 cups hot water
Salt
Pepper
½ cup grated American
cheese
1 round steak of venison,
tenderized
1 egg, beaten
½ cup all-purpose flour
Mozzarella cheese slices
1 12-ounce package egg
noodles, cooked

- Preheat oven to 350 degrees.
- In a large skillet, sauté onion in ½ cup of the oil until tender. Stir in tomato paste, garlic, and water. Season with salt and pepper to taste. Heat thoroughly. Add grated cheese, stirring until cheese is melted. Set aside.
- Cut steak into serving pieces. Dip into egg; dredge in flour. Brown in the remaining 3 tablespoons oil. Drain well.
- Place venison in a greased 9 by 13-inch baking dish. Cover with the tomato mixture. Bake, covered, for 45 minutes.
- Uncover; place a slice of cheese on each piece. Bake for an additional 3 minutes. Serve over egg noodles.

Yield: 8 servings

Note: Have your butcher tenderize the round steak, or do it yourself by pounding with a meat cleaver.

Venison Pepper Steak

**2 pounds venison
backstrap or tenderloin
4 tablespoons soy sauce
1 large onion, sliced into
rings
1 bell pepper, sliced into
rings
1 tablespoon vegetable oil
Celery salt
Black pepper
1 cup canned tomatoes,
drained and chopped
4 beef bouillon cubes
1 cup hot water
2 tablespoons cornstarch
Hot cooked rice**

• Cut venison into narrow strips. Marinate in soy sauce in a shallow glass dish for 2 to 3 hours or overnight.

• In a large skillet or Dutch oven, sauté onion and bell pepper in hot oil until vegetables are tender. Remove from pan; sauté marinated meat strips in same pan until meat begins to brown.

• Add sautéed onion and bell pepper. Stir in celery salt, black pepper, and tomatoes.

• Dissolve bouillon cubes in hot water; stir in cornstarch. Pour over top of meat mixture. Add enough water to cover. Simmer 30 to 40 minutes or until tender. Serve over rice.

Yield: 10 servings

Venison Hot Tamales

2 pounds ground venison
or ground beef
2 medium onions, finely
chopped
2 cloves garlic, finely
chopped
½ cup water
1 tablespoon salt
1½ teaspoons red pepper
½ cup cornmeal
1 8-ounce can tomato
sauce
3 tablespoons chili powder
Tamale papers (see note
for address of supplier)

Meal Mixture

2 cups cornmeal
3 teaspoons salt
1 teaspoon red pepper

Sauce

1 8-ounce can tomato
sauce
2 tablespoons chili powder
1 tablespoon salt
3 cups water

- In a mixing bowl, combine the venison or beef, onion, garlic, water, salt, red pepper, cornmeal, tomato sauce, and chili powder, mixing well. Set aside.

- Soak tamale papers in water until pliable.

- Mix together the cornmeal, salt, and red pepper. Place 1 teaspoon cornmeal mixture on tamale paper followed by a roll of meat mixture. Add more Meal Mixture to top of meat and roll in paper, closing one end and leaving one end of paper open. Tie loosely in bundles of 3 tamales. Place in a Dutch oven or stock pot with open end up. Weight with a saucer to keep tamales from rising while cooking.

- To make the Sauce, combine tomato sauce, chili powder, salt, and 3 cups of water in a saucepan. Bring to a boil; pour over hot tamales. Add additional water to bring sauce level one inch below top of tamales. Simmer 1½ hours. Place tamales and a little of the sauce in a zip-top plastic bag; freeze.

Yield: 50 tamales

Note: The hot tamale papers may be purchased from:

Rainbow Paper Company
P. O. Box 9985
New Iberia, Louisiana 70562-9985
Phone: (318) 369-9007

Dove and Sausage Gumbo

15 dove breasts
1 10½-ounce can
consommé
1 beef-flavored bouillon
cube
½ cup vegetable oil
½ cup all-purpose flour
1½ cups finely chopped
onion
2 stalks celery, finely
chopped
2 tablespoons
Worcestershire sauce
2 cloves garlic, minced
1 to 2 bay leaves
½ teaspoon dried whole
basil
¼ teaspoon poultry
seasoning
¼ teaspoon freshly ground
pepper
⅛ teaspoon ground red
pepper
⅛ teaspoon ground allspice
⅛ teaspoon ground cloves
¾ pound smoked sausage,
cut into ¼-inch slices
¼ cup dry red wine
⅛ teaspoon hot sauce
Hot cooked rice

• Place dove breasts in Dutch oven, and cover with water. Boil about 20 minutes. Cool and remove meat from bones. Reserve cooking liquid in Dutch oven, adding water if necessary to make 2¼ cups liquid. Set meat aside.

• Add consommé and bouillon cube to Dutch oven. Cook until bouillon cube is dissolved.

• Brown dove in hot oil in a large skillet; drain well. Pour off all but ¼ cup oil. Add flour to reserved oil; cook over medium heat, stirring constantly, until roux is the color of a copper penny (about 10 to 15 minutes).

• Gradually add about 1½ cups of consommé mixture to roux; cook over medium heat, stirring constantly, until thickened and bubbly. Stir in onion and celery, and cook about 5 minutes or until vegetables are tender. Add roux mixture to remaining consommé mixture, and stir well. Stir in Worcestershire sauce and seasonings.

• Brown sausage, and drain well. Stir sausage and dove into roux mixture; simmer 1½ hours, stirring occasionally. Add wine and hot sauce; stir well. Remove bay leaves, and serve gumbo over rice.

Yield: about 1¾ quarts

225

Grilled Doves

12 dove breasts
½ cup Italian dressing
½ cup Dale's seasoning
Garlic powder
Black pepper
6 jalapeño peppers,
  halved and seeded
6 slices bacon, halved

- In a shallow glass dish, combine Italian dressing and Dale's seasoning, mixing well. Place dove breasts in mixture, turning once. Marinate in refrigerator overnight.

- Season doves with garlic powder and black pepper. Place one pepper half in dove cavity and wrap dove with bacon half, securing with a toothpick. Repeat for remaining doves.

- Grill doves over medium coals 20 minutes, turning occasionally.

Yield: 3 to 4 servings

Smothered Doves

1 cup all-purpose flour
Salt
Pepper
½ teaspoon crushed
  rosemary leaves
12 to 15 dove breasts
3 tablespoons butter or
  vegetable oil
1 large onion, sliced
1 cup water
1 cup dry red wine
Hot cooked rice

- Combine flour, salt, pepper, and rosemary leaves in a brown paper bag; add dove breasts and shake to coat evenly.

- In a heavy Dutch oven, brown coated breasts in butter or oil. Place onion slices on top and pour water over all. Cover and simmer slowly for 30 to 45 minutes. (More water may be added if needed to prevent sticking.)

- Pour wine over birds; cook an additional 5 to 10 minutes. Serve over rice.

Yield: 3 to 4 servings

Doves Au Vin

24 doves
Salt
Pepper
¼ pound (1 stick) butter
1 small onion, minced
1 8-ounce can sliced
 mushrooms, reserving
 liquid
2 cups dry white wine
½ cup sherry
1 10¾-ounce can
 consommé

• Sprinkle doves lightly with salt and pepper. Sauté doves in butter until brown on all sides. Remove doves and set aside.

• Add onion to pan drippings. Sauté until clear. Stir in mushrooms and liquid, wines, and consommé. Stir to loosen pan drippings; simmer for 5 minutes.

• Return doves to pan. Cover and simmer for 30 minutes or until tender.

Yield: 8 servings

Baked Doves

1 16-ounce bottle Italian
 dressing
½ cup Worcestershire
 sauce
20 doves
20 slices bacon

• In a small bowl, combine dressing and Worcestershire sauce. Place doves in a shallow baking dish; pour in dressing mixture; cover. Marinate in refrigerator overnight.

• Preheat oven to 350 degrees.

• Remove doves from marinade. Wrap each dove with bacon slice, securing with a toothpick. Return doves to baking dish; baste with marinade.

• Bake, covered, for 1 hour. Broil for a few minutes to crisp bacon.

Yield: 5 to 6 servings

Roast Duck

3 mallards for roasting
Salt
Pepper
4 oranges, peeled and
  quartered
2½ cups beef bouillon
1 bay leaf
Cornstarch
Water
½ to ¾ cup red wine, such
  as Merlot
1 6-ounce jar Bing cherry
  preserves

• Preheat oven to 325 degrees.
• Wash mallards well and pat dry. Season with salt and pepper. Fill duck cavities with oranges; place in roasting pan. Pour in bouillon; add bay leaf. Bake, covered, 2½ hours.
• Remove oranges and discard. Halve ducks and place on warming rack. Bring pan drippings in roasting pan to a boil. Thicken with a mixture of cornstarch and water. Pour in wine; add preserves, stirring to make a thick sauce. Serve over ducks.

Yield: 6 servings

Tar Baby's Ducks

6 tablespoons all-purpose
  flour
1 1¼-ounce can paprika
1 tablespoon Creole
  seasoning
2 tablespoons sugar
2 tablespoons Accent
3 14-ounce cans chicken
  broth
Salt
Pepper
3 wild ducks, dressed
12 bay leaves
Hot cooked wild rice

• Preheat oven to 350 degrees.
• In a large mixing bowl, combine the flour, paprika, Creole seasoning, sugar, and Accent. Add chicken broth; stir until blended.
• Salt and pepper ducks to taste; place four bay leaves in each cavity. Place ducks breast down in a Dutch oven; cover with broth mixture.
• Bake, covered, for 2½ hours or until tender. Debone ducks, and serve with gravy over rice.

Yield: 6 servings

Wild Duck Casserole

2 large ducks
3 stalks celery
1 onion, halved plus
½ cup, chopped
1½ teaspoons salt
¼ teaspoon pepper
1 4-ounce can mushrooms,
drained (reserving juice)
¼ pound (1 stick) butter
½ cup all-purpose flour
1 6-ounce package long
grain and wild rice,
cooked
1 tablespoon parsley
1½ cups half-and-half
½ cup sliced almonds,
lightly toasted

- Cook ducks in water seasoned with celery, halved onion, salt, and pepper until tender. Remove duck, reserving broth. Debone and cut in bite-size pieces.

- Strain duck broth; add to mushroom juice to make 1½ cups.

- Preheat oven to 350 degrees.

- Sauté chopped onion in butter for 1 minute; add flour and stir. Add mushrooms, stirring constantly, and gradually stir in mushroom-broth mixture. Cook until smooth and thick. Stir in duck, rice, parsley, and half-and-half, stirring constantly until smooth. Pour into 2-quart greased baking dish; cover with almonds.

- Bake, covered, for 20 minutes; remove cover and continue to bake 6 to 8 minutes, or until browned.

Yield: 6 to 8 servings

Brandied Duck Breasts with Wild Rice

1 cup uncooked wild rice
¼ pound (1 stick) butter
4 duck breasts
⅓ cup brandy
⅓ cup sherry
1 tablespoon
  Worcestershire sauce
4 tablespoons grape jelly
2 teaspoons cornstarch
2 teaspoons cold water

- Cook rice according to package directions.

- Melt butter in skillet; brown duck breasts quickly. Remove duck breasts from skillet. Stir in brandy, sherry, Worcestershire sauce, and grape jelly. Bring to a boil, stirring to dissolve the jelly.

- Add the duck breasts. Cover; reduce heat to low. Simmer 20 minutes, turning duck breasts once. Remove duck breasts from pan.

- Blend cornstarch in cold water and stir until smooth; add to liquid in skillet. Stir until thickened.

- To serve, spoon sauce over duck breasts and wild rice.

Yield: 4 servings

Gumbo (Seafood or Duck)

⅔ cup oil
⅔ cup all-purpose flour
2 large onions, chopped
1 large bell pepper,
    chopped
3 cloves garlic, minced
3 ribs celery, chopped
2 cups red wine
3 tablespoons
    Worcestershire sauce
2 tablespoons parsley
2 bay leaves
2 tablespoons salt
1½ teaspoons black
    pepper
⅛ teaspoon red pepper
1 tablespoon thyme
2 quarts water or stock
1 28-ounce can tomatoes
1 16-ounce package sliced
    okra
3 to 4 tablespoons gumbo
    filé
Tabasco
Seafood or duck—see
    Variation
Hot cooked rice

- In a large Dutch oven or stock pot, make roux with oil and flour until golden or dark brown. Add onion, bell pepper, garlic, and celery. Cook over low heat until softened (10 to 12 minutes).

- Add wine, Worcestershire sauce, parsley, bay leaves, salt, black pepper, red pepper, and thyme; mix well.

- Stir in water or stock, tomatoes, and okra. Add filé to mixture 5 minutes before serving. Remove bay leaves. Add Tabasco to taste, and serve over rice.

Yield: 1 gallon

Variation: For seafood gumbo, add one fillet of ocean fish when adding water. Cook until tender. Stir in 1 pound peeled shrimp and ¹/₂ pound crabmeat and/or oysters, which add a good flavor. Simmer, stirring frequently. Serve over rice.

For duck gumbo, boil duck in Creole seasoning or crab boil (whole ducks for several hours, duck breasts for 2 hours); debone. Pour off broth and discard. Add 2 quarts water to duck, bring to another boil. Use this broth instead of water for duck gumbo.

231

Grilled Quail

16 quail, dressed
16 jalapeño peppers
16 slices bacon
1 8-ounce bottle Italian
   salad dressing
½ cup Chablis or other dry
   white wine
⅓ cup soy sauce
¼ cup lemon juice
¼ teaspoon pepper
Banana peppers for
   garnish, optional

• Rinse quail thoroughly with cold water; pat dry. Place a jalapeño pepper into quail cavity. Wrap 1 bacon slice around each quail; secure with a toothpick. Place quail in a large shallow dish.

• Combine Italian salad dressing, wine, soy sauce, lemon juice, and pepper; pour over quail. Cover and marinate in refrigerator 8 hours. Remove quail from dish, reserving marinade. Boil marinade in a small saucepan for 5 minutes. Set aside.

• Prepare charcoal fire in one end of grill; let burn 15 to 20 minutes or until flames disappear and coals are white. Grill quail, covered, on opposite end 1 hour, turning once, and basting often with marinade. Garnish with banana peppers, if desired.

Yield: 8 servings

Note: You may bake quail on rack of a roasting pan in the oven at 350 degrees for 1 hour, turning once, and basting often with marinade.

Baked Pecan Catfish

1 cup buttermilk
1 egg, beaten
1 cup flour
1 tablespoon salt
1 tablespoon paprika
⅛ teaspoon pepper
1 cup ground pecans
¼ cup sesame seeds
2 pounds catfish fillets,
  preferably 5 to 7 ounces
  each
½ cup butter, melted
¼ cup pecan halves
Lemon wedges
Parsley sprigs

- Preheat oven to 350 degrees.
- Combine buttermilk with egg. In another bowl, sift together flour, salt, paprika, and pepper. Add ground pecans and sesame seeds. Add dry ingredients to milk and egg mixture. Blend well. Dip fish in batter, coating well.
- Pour butter into a 9 by 13-inch baking dish. Place battered fish in dish and put pecan halves on top.
- Bake for 30 minutes, or until fish is golden brown and flakes easily. Garnish with lemon wedges and parsley.

Yield: 5 to 7 servings

Note: May be made ahead of time and baked when needed.

Catfish Parmesan

6 pan dressed whole
   catfish or catfish fillets
2 cups dry bread crumbs
¾ cup Parmesan cheese
¼ cup chopped parsley
1 teaspoon paprika
½ teaspoon oregano
¼ teaspoon basil
2 teaspoons salt
½ teaspoon pepper
¾ cup butter, melted, or
   cooking oil
Lemon wedges

- Preheat oven to 375 degrees.
- Combine bread crumbs, Parmesan cheese, parsley, paprika, oregano, basil, salt and pepper. Dip catfish in melted butter or oil and roll in crumb mixture.
- Arrange fish in a well greased 9 by 13-inch baking dish. Bake for 25 minutes or until fish flakes easily. Cooking time will be less if using fillets. Garnish with lemon wedges.

Yield: 6 servings

Classic Fried Catfish

¾ cup yellow cornmeal
¼ cup flour
2 teaspoons salt
1 teaspoon ground red
   pepper
¼ teaspoon garlic powder
4 catfish fillets or whole
   catfish
Vegetable oil

- Combine cornmeal, flour, salt, ground red pepper, and garlic powder. Coat catfish with mixture, shaking off excess.
- Fill deep pot or 12-inch skillet half full with vegetable oil. Heat to 350 degrees.
- Add catfish in a single layer, and fry until golden brown, about 5 to 6 minutes, depending on size. Remove and drain on paper towels.

Yield: 4 servings

Broiled Catfish

4 catfish fillets
½ teaspoon garlic salt
½ teaspoon lemon pepper

Mustard-Dill Sauce

2 tablespoons butter
2 tablespoons flour
1¼ cups milk
¼ cup chopped parsley
¼ cup chopped fresh dill or
1 teaspoon dried dillweed
3 tablespoons Dijon
mustard
¼ teaspoon salt

- Sprinkle catfish with garlic salt and lemon pepper. Preheat broiler.
- Place fish on the greased rack of an unheated broiler pan. Tuck under any thin edges.
- Broil 3 inches from the heat for 4 to 6 minutes or until fish flakes easily with a fork.
- To prepare the Mustard-Dill Sauce, melt butter in a small saucepan. Stir in flour. Add milk all at once. Cook and stir until thickened and bubbly. Cook and stir 1 minute more.
- Add parsley, dill, mustard, and salt, mixing well.

Yield: 4 servings with 1½ cups sauce.

Crawfish Étouffée

½ pound (2 sticks) butter
1 cup flour
3 cups chopped onion
3 cups chopped bell pepper
3 cups chopped celery
4 cloves garlic, minced
4 14½-ounce cans chicken
broth
½ cup chopped parsley
2 teaspoons salt
1 teaspoon black pepper
½ teaspoon ground red
pepper
3 pounds peeled crawfish
tails
Hot rice

- Make a roux by melting butter in a large stockpot or Dutch oven; stir in flour and brown on medium heat until a caramel color.
- Add onion, bell pepper, celery, and garlic; stir and cook 5 minutes.
- Mix in chicken broth, parsley, salt, black pepper, and red pepper. Cook until vegetables are tender.
- Stir in crawfish tails; simmer 20 minutes, stirring often. Serve over hot rice.

Yield: 12 to 15 servings

235

Shrimp and Crawfish Jambalaya

2 tablespoons flour
2 tablespoons vegetable oil
or bacon drippings
2 onions, chopped
½ cup chopped green
onions
¾ cup chopped bell pepper
1½ teaspoons minced
garlic
1 cup chopped celery
3½ cups water, divided
1 8-ounce can tomato
sauce
1 10-ounce can tomatoes
with green chiles
1 pound crawfish tails and
fat
1 pound shrimp, peeled
and cleaned
½ cup fresh parsley,
chopped
½ teaspoon thyme
¾ teaspoon oregano
1½ cups uncooked rice
Salt
Ground red pepper
Black pepper

- In a large stockpot or Dutch oven, make a roux with the flour and oil; brown on medium heat until it is a light brown caramel color.

- Add onions, bell pepper, garlic, and celery. Simmer 5 minutes. Pour in 1½ cups of the water, tomato sauce, and tomatoes. Simmer for 30 minutes.

- Stir in the crawfish tails, fat, and shrimp; cook 10 to 15 minutes. Add the remaining 2 cups water and all remaining ingredients. Stir and cook on low heat, covered, for about 30 minutes or until rice is tender. Remove from heat and let sit for about 5 minutes before serving.

Yield: 8 to 10 servings

Shrimp and Asparagus Casserole

¾ cup butter, divided
½ cup flour
3 cups half-and-half
1½ cups milk
½ cup sherry
¾ cup grated sharp
  Cheddar cheese
½ cup grated Parmesan
  cheese
1 lemon, juiced
1½ tablespoons grated
  onion
1 tablespoon chopped
  parsley
1 tablespoon prepared
  mustard
2½ teaspoons salt
Pepper
1 cup mayonnaise
1 pound fresh mushrooms,
  sliced
¾ pound vermicelli, cooked
  and drained
2 pounds shrimp, cooked,
  peeled, and deveined
2 15-ounce cans
  asparagus, drained

- In a heavy saucepan, melt ½ cup of the butter. Blend in flour. Cook 2 minutes. Add half-and-half, milk, and sherry. Cook until thickened, stirring constantly.

- Add cheeses, lemon juice, onion, parsley, mustard, and salt. Season with pepper. Heat until cheeses are melted. Remove from heat. Add mayonnaise.

- Preheat oven to 350 degrees.

- Sauté mushrooms in the remaining ¼ cup butter until tender. Set aside.

- Combine sauce, vermicelli, and shrimp. Mix well.

- In two greased 2-quart baking dishes, arrange layers in the following order: ⅓ of the shrimp mixture, ½ of the sautéed mushrooms, and ½ of the asparagus. Repeat layers, ending with the shrimp.

- Bake, uncovered, for 30 minutes, or until thoroughly heated.

Yield: 10 to 12 servings

237

Shrimp Creole

¼ **cup vegetable oil**
¼ **cup flour**
1½ **cups chopped onion**
1 **cup chopped green onions**
1 **cup chopped celery**
1 **cup chopped bell pepper**
2 **cloves garlic, minced**
1 **16-ounce can chopped tomatoes, undrained**
1 **8-ounce can tomato sauce**
1 **6-ounce can tomato paste**
1½ **cups water**
1 **tablespoon lemon juice**
1½ **teaspoons salt**
1 **teaspoon black pepper**
1 **teaspoon Worcestershire sauce**
½ **teaspoon ground red pepper**
⅛ **teaspoon hot sauce**
2 **to 3 bay leaves**
5 **pounds large fresh shrimp, peeled and deveined**
2 **10-ounce packages saffron yellow rice mix**
½ **cup finely chopped fresh parsley**

- Combine oil and flour in a Dutch oven; cook over medium heat, stirring constantly, until roux is chocolate colored (about 15 minutes). Stir in onion, green onions, celery, bell pepper, and garlic; cook 15 minutes or until vegetables are tender, stirring frequently.

- Stir in tomatoes, tomato sauce, tomato paste, water, lemon juice, salt, black pepper, Worcestershire sauce, red pepper, hot sauce, and bay leaves. Bring to a boil; cover, reduce heat, and simmer 1 hour, stirring occasionally.

- Add shrimp to tomato mixture. Bring to a boil; cover, reduce heat, and simmer 10 minutes or until shrimp turn pink. Remove and discard bay leaves.

- Prepare rice mix according to package directions. Serve shrimp mixture over rice; sprinkle with chopped parsley.

Yield: 10 servings

Shrimp Scampi

**2 pounds unpeeled large
  fresh shrimp**
¼ pound (1 stick) butter
½ cup olive oil
2 tablespoons lemon juice
**4 large cloves garlic,
  minced**
**1 medium onion, finely
  chopped**
½ teaspoon dried tarragon
½ teaspoon steak sauce
**½ teaspoon
  Worcestershire sauce**
¼ teaspoon hot sauce
1 teaspoon salt
**Freshly ground black
  pepper**
**4 tablespoons finely
  chopped parsley**
Lemon quarters

- Peel shrimp, leaving tail segment. Butterfly shrimp and remove vein. Wash under cold water and pat dry.

- Preheat broiler.

- Melt butter in shallow dish large enough to hold shrimp in one layer. Do not let butter brown. Stir in olive oil, lemon juice, garlic, onion, tarragon, steak sauce, Worcestershire sauce, hot sauce, salt, pepper, and shrimp, turning until coated with the sauce.

- Broil 3 to 4 inches from heat for 5 minutes. Turn and broil 5 minutes more, or until lightly browned. Do not overcook. Sprinkle with parsley and garnish with lemon quarters.

Yield: 6 servings

Shrimp Spaghetti

**3 pounds shrimp, peeled
and deveined**
1 tablespoon lemon juice
1½ cups butter, melted
**1 tablespoon
Worcestershire sauce**
1 teaspoon salt
1 tablespoon black pepper
½ teaspoon basil
½ teaspoon thyme
¼ teaspoon garlic powder
1 tablespoon parsley flakes
**8 ounces processed cheese
loaf, cubed**
**12 ounces spaghetti,
cooked al dente**

- Preheat oven to 350 degrees.
- In a 3-quart casserole, combine the shrimp, lemon juice, butter, Worcestershire sauce, salt, pepper, basil, thyme, garlic powder, and parsley flakes; cook in oven for 25 minutes. Stir occasionally.
- Stir cheese into hot shrimp mixture, stirring until cheese melts. Add spaghetti, mixing well. (May be prepared to this point and refrigerated until ready to use.)
- Return to oven to reheat, completely melting the cheese.

Yield: 6 to 8 servings

Note: Cooked chicken may be substituted for the shrimp.

Shrimp Aurora

2 tablespoons butter,
melted
2 tablespoons white wine
Garlic salt
2 pounds medium
(26-30 count) shrimp,
peeled and deveined
1 16-ounce package angel
hair pasta, cooked al
dente and kept warm

Hollandaise Sauce

½ pound (2 sticks) butter,
divided
3 egg yolks
1 tablespoon cold water
1 tablespoon lemon juice
Dash of salt
White pepper

- Preheat broiler to 450 degrees.
- Combine butter and wine; season with garlic salt to taste. Pour over shrimp and toss well. Place shrimp in a greased 9 by 13-inch baking dish in a single layer.
- Broil 10 minutes or until shrimp turn pink.
- Meanwhile, boil pasta according to package directions. Drain well and keep warm.
- To make Hollandaise Sauce, melt ¾ cup of the butter; set aside.
- Beat egg yolks until thick. Place yolks in top of double boiler; add water, lemon juice, and salt. Beat well; place over simmering water. Add 1 tablespoon of the remaining butter; stir with wire whisk until thick enough to see bottom of pan between strokes, about 5 minutes. Remove pan from hot water; beat in remaining 3 tablespoons of the butter. Pour melted butter into mixture, very slowly, beating constantly. (If sauce curdles, beat in 1 tablespoon cold water.) Add white pepper.
- Serve baked shrimp over warm pasta and top with Hollandaise Sauce.

Yield: 6 to 8 servings

Note: Hollandaise sauce will keep in refrigerator for several days, or will freeze well. Thaw and let sauce reach room temperature.

Fiery Cajun Shrimp

½ pound (2 sticks) butter, melted
½ cup Worcestershire sauce
4 tablespoons ground black pepper
1 teaspoon rosemary leaves
2 teaspoons hot sauce
2 teaspoons salt
3 cloves garlic, minced
6 lemons, 2 juiced and 4 sliced
5 to 6 pounds shrimp, peeled and deveined

- Preheat oven to 400 degrees.
- In a bowl, mix the butter, Worcestershire sauce, black pepper, rosemary, hot sauce, salt, garlic, and lemon juice. Pour about ½ cup sauce to cover the bottom of a 9 by 13-inch baking dish.
- Arrange layers of shrimp and lemon slices until 1 inch from the top of the dish. Pour remaining sauce over the shrimp and lemon slices.
- Bake, uncovered, stirring once or twice until the shrimp turn pink, about 15 to 20 minutes. Serve with toasted French bread.

Yield: 8 to 10 servings

Grilled Bacon-Wrapped Shrimp

1 16-ounce bottle Italian dressing
1 cup Basting Sauce*
¼ teaspoon garlic powder
2 pounds large shrimp, peeled and deveined
1 pound bacon, cut in 3-inch strips
Dry seasoning rub

- In a mixing bowl, combine dressing, basting sauce, and garlic powder.
- Wrap shrimp in bacon strips and secure with a toothpick. Marinate in dressing mixture for 2 hours.
- Place shrimp over medium-hot coals; sprinkle with seasoning rub. Turn when bacon begins to sizzle; sprinkle with seasoning rub again. Grill until shrimp turn pink and bacon is crispy.

*Refer to Basting Sauce on page 261 in Sauce Section.

Yield: 4 to 6 servings

Shrimp Fettuccine

3 onions, chopped
2 bell peppers, chopped
3 stalks celery, chopped
3 cloves garlic, finely
  chopped
4 teaspoons dried parsley
¾ pound (3 sticks) butter,
  melted
¼ cup flour
1 pint half-and-half
⅓ cup evaporated milk
1 8-ounce Mexican
  processed cheese loaf,
  diced
3 pounds shrimp, boiled
  with seasoning
1 pound fettuccine, cooked
  al dente and drained
Grated cheese for topping

- Preheat oven to 350 degrees.
- In a large Dutch oven, sauté onions, peppers, celery, garlic, and parsley in butter for 10 minutes or until tender. Stir in flour, mixing well.
- Add half-and-half, milk, and cheese. Simmer for 15 to 20 minutes, stirring occasionally to make a smooth sauce. Fold in shrimp.
- Combine fettuccine with the shrimp sauce. Pour into a greased 9 by 13-inch baking dish. Top with grated cheese. Bake for 45 minutes, or until bubbly and thoroughly heated.

Yield: 8 to 10 servings

Shrimp-Stuffed Eggplant

2 medium eggplants
½ cup chopped onion
⅓ cup chopped celery
1 clove garlic, minced
1 pound medium-size fresh
  shrimp, peeled and
  deveined
2½ tablespoons butter,
  melted
⅓ cup plus 2 tablespoons
  Italian-seasoned
  breadcrumbs, divided
¼ teaspoon garlic powder
¼ teaspoon celery salt
⅛ teaspoon ground red
  pepper

- Cut eggplants in half lengthwise. Remove pulp, leaving a ¼ to ½-inch shell; set shells aside. Chop pulp.

- Preheat oven to 350 degrees.

- Cook onion, celery, garlic, and eggplant pulp in 1 tablespoon of the butter in a large skillet over medium-high heat, stirring constantly, 10 to 12 minutes or until tender. Add shrimp; cook, stirring constantly, 3 to 5 minutes or until shrimp turn pink. Remove from heat; stir in ⅓ cup of the breadcrumbs, the garlic powder, celery salt, and red pepper.

- Place eggplant shells on a baking sheet; spoon hot mixture into shells. Sprinkle with the remaining 2 tablespoons of the breadcrumbs; dot with the remaining 1½ tablespoons of the butter. Bake for 20 to 25 minutes.

Yield: 4 servings

Marinated Shrimp

2 bay leaves
1 teaspoon ground red
pepper
1 tablespoon celery seed
¾ cup salt (may use less)
Water
6 pounds fresh shrimp

Marinade

2 cups vegetable oil
½ cup ketchup
3 tablespoons lemon juice
¼ cup apple cider vinegar
1 tablespoon
Worcestershire sauce
1 5-ounce jar horseradish
1 5-ounce jar hot Creole
mustard
1 cup thinly sliced yellow
onions
Salt
Pepper

- In a large stockpot, combine bay leaves, red pepper, celery seed, and salt with enough water to boil the shrimp. Bring to a boil over high heat; toss in shrimp and return to a boil. Cook until shrimp turn pink and rise to the top. Let stand for 1 minute. Drain and cool; peel and devein shrimp.

- To make the Marinade, combine all of the ingredients, mixing well. Add cooked shrimp and marinate in the refrigerator for at least 24 hours.

Yield: 10 to 12 servings

Marinated Shrimp with Capers

1 lemon, sliced
Salt
Pepper
Celery salt
Garlic salt
1 clove garlic, halved
Water
5 pounds fresh shrimp
2½ cups vegetable oil
1½ cups vinegar
5 teaspoons celery seed
Dash of Tabasco
1 tablespoon prepared
    mustard
1 tablespoon salt
1 tablespoon pepper
½ teaspoon Accent
½ teaspoon garlic salt
¼ cup Worcestershire
    sauce
1 3¼-ounce jar capers and
    juice
4 medium onions, thinly
    sliced
2 14-ounce cans artichoke
    hearts
1 box bay leaves

• In a large stockpot, combine lemon slices, salt, pepper, celery salt, garlic salt, and garlic clove with enough water to boil shrimp. Bring to a boil, stir in shrimp, and cook until shrimp turn pink. Let stand in water for 1 minute. Drain and cool shrimp; peel and devein. Set aside.

• In a large saucepan, combine oil, vinegar, celery seed, Tabasco, prepared mustard, salt, pepper, Accent, garlic salt, Worcestershire sauce, and capers and juice. Heat and stir until mustard blends with other ingredients. Set aside.

• In a glass serving dish, arrange layer of shrimp, onion, artichoke hearts, and bay leaves. Repeat until all are used. Pour marinade over layers; marinate in refrigerator for at least 24 hours. Stir occasionally. Drain juice before serving. Serve chilled.

Yield: 8 to 10 servings

Grilled Shrimp-and-Scallop Kabobs

**30 unpeeled, jumbo fresh
shrimp**
30 sea scallops
1 cup olive oil
½ cup fresh lime juice
2 cloves garlic, crushed
½ teaspoon salt
**¼ teaspoon freshly ground
pepper**

- Peel shrimp, leaving tails intact, and devein. Combine shrimp and scallops in a shallow dish.

- Combine olive oil and remaining ingredients; pour over shrimp and scallops. Cover and refrigerate 1 hour, stirring occasionally.

- Remove shrimp and scallops from marinade, discarding marinade. Alternate shrimp and scallops on ten 14-inch wooden skewers that have been soaked in water to prevent burning.

- Grill, uncovered, over medium coals (300 to 350 degrees) 8 to 10 minutes on each side.

Yield: 10 servings

Note: Cooking time may vary according to size of shrimp and scallops. They may be cooked on separate skewers to control the degree of doneness, if desired.

Lobster Thermidor

2½ pounds boiled lobster
   meat, cubed
3 tablespoons butter,
   melted
1 8-ounce can mushrooms,
   drained
½ cup sherry
¼ teaspoon salt
¼ teaspoon paprika
2 tablespoons flour
2 cups light cream
2 egg yolks, beaten
1 10¾-ounce can cream of
   potato soup
Grated cheese

- In a 4-quart saucepan, briefly sauté lobster in butter. Stir in mushrooms, sherry, salt, and paprika. Sprinkle with flour and stir.
- Gradually add cream, egg yolks, and soup; simmer until thick, about 2 minutes.
- Place in chafing dish and sprinkle with cheese. Serve in patty shells or over rice.

Yield: 6 to 8 servings

Note: Shrimp or a combination of shrimp and lobster may be substituted for the lobster.

Crab Cakes

2 cups mayonnaise, divided
½ cup Dijon mustard
½ cup honey
1 cup bread crumbs
¼ cup crushed saltine
  crackers
1 lemon, juiced
1 egg white
1 tablespoon chopped
  parsley
1 pound jumbo lump
  crabmeat, cleaned
½ cup clarified butter

- To make sauce, mix 1 cup of the mayonnaise, mustard, and the honey in a mixing bowl. Refrigerate for 1 hour to let flavors blend. Set aside.

- For the crab cakes, combine the remaining 1 cup mayonnaise, bread crumbs, crushed crackers, lemon juice, egg white, parsley, and crabmeat, being careful not to break up the lumps of crab. Form into cakes; sauté in clarified butter until each side is golden brown. Drain well.

- To serve, put sauce on individual serving plates and top with a crab cake.

Yield: 4 to 6 servings

Note: To clarify butter, place butter in top of a double boiler over hot water. Position over low heat just until butter has melted. When the milky sediment has separated from the clear liquid, pour off the clear liquid, which is the clarified butter. Discard the milky sediment.

Crab Pies

1 large onion, cut in
chunks
1 large bell pepper, cut in
chunks
2 ribs celery, cut in chunks
¼ pound (1 stick) butter,
melted
1 10-ounce can tomatoes
with chiles
1 10¾-ounce can golden
cream of mushroom
soup
1 pound crabmeat,
cleaned
8 ounces Cheddar cheese,
grated
Salt
Pepper
24 4-inch pie shells,
unbaked or 2 9-inch pie
shells, unbaked

- Put onion, bell pepper, and celery in a food processor; process until finely chopped. In a large skillet, sauté processed vegetables in butter; cook on low heat for 20 minutes.
- Pour tomatoes and soup in processor; process until smooth. Add tomato mixture to vegetables and simmer for 20 minutes.
- Preheat oven to 350 degrees.
- Stir in crabmeat; cook for an additional 15 minutes. Sprinkle with cheese; stir until melted. Season with salt and pepper to taste. Cool and spoon into pie shells.
- Bake for 30 minutes or until golden brown.

Yield: 24 individual pies

Glazed Teriyaki Salmon

⅓ **cup orange juice**
⅓ **cup soy sauce**
¼ **cup dry white wine**
2 **tablespoons vegetable oil**
1 **tablespoon grated fresh ginger**
1 **teaspoon dry mustard**
1 **teaspoon lemon juice**
Dash of sugar
1 **garlic clove, minced**
½ **teaspoon freshly ground black pepper**
4 **4 to 6-ounce salmon fillets**

- Combine orange juice, soy sauce, wine, vegetable oil, ginger, mustard, lemon juice, sugar, garlic, and black pepper in a shallow dish or large heavy-duty, zip-top plastic bag; add salmon. Cover or seal; chill 30 minutes, turning once.
- Preheat oven to 400 degrees.
- Remove fish fillets from marinade, reserving marinade. Place fish in a 9 by 13-inch pan.
- Bake 20 to 25 minutes, or until fish flakes easily with a fork.
- Bring marinade to boil in a small saucepan; boil 5 minutes, stirring occasionally. Serve with salmon.

Yield: 4 servings

Oyster Rockefeller Casserole

4 dozen small oysters
3 10-ounce packages
frozen chopped spinach
¾ pound (3 sticks) butter
1 teaspoon thyme
1⅔ cups chopped green
onions
1 cup chopped celery
1 large clove garlic,
crushed
1 tablespoon
Worcestershire sauce
1 teaspoon anchovy paste
1½ cups seasoned bread
crumbs
¾ cup chopped parsley
½ cup freshly grated
Parmesan cheese
½ teaspoon salt
¼ teaspoon black pepper
¼ teaspoon ground red
pepper

- Drain oysters, reserving liquid, and chop. Set aside.

- In a saucepan, prepare spinach according to package directions, drain, and set aside.

- Preheat oven to 375 degrees.

- In a large skillet over moderate heat, melt butter and add thyme, green onion, celery, and garlic. Sauté for 5 minutes. Add Worcestershire sauce, anchovy paste, and bread crumbs. Stir well for 5 minutes until bread crumbs are toasted.

- Gently stir in oysters, ½ cup of reserved oyster liquid, parsley, and cheese. Cook for 3 minutes or until oysters curl. Add spinach and season with salt, pepper, and red pepper. Pour into greased 3-quart casserole and bake for 20 to 25 minutes.

Yield: 10 servings

Trout Amandine

4 to 6 trout fillets
Salt
Pepper
3 eggs, slightly beaten
2 cups milk
Flour for dredging
Hot oil
1 lemon, juiced
Toasted almonds

Parsley-Butter Sauce

¼ pound (1 stick) butter, melted
¼ teaspoon salt
¼ teaspoon white pepper
1 teaspoon chopped fresh parsley

• Season trout with salt and pepper to taste. Combine eggs with milk. Dip seasoned fillets into egg mixture; dredge in flour. Sauté trout in hot oil until golden. Remove with a slotted spoon; drain well. Keep warm.

• To prepare sauce, combine butter, salt, white pepper, and parsley, mixing well.

• Sprinkle top of warm trout with sauce, lemon juice, and almonds.

Yield: 4 to 6 servings

253

Beer Batter

2 eggs, separated
4 tablespoons butter, melted
3 teaspoons salt
1 cup cornstarch
½ cup flour
⅔ cup beer

- Beat egg yolks. Add butter, salt, cornstarch, flour, and beer, mixing well to smooth consistency.
- Beat egg whites until soft peaks are formed; fold into batter.

Note: This batter is great for shrimp.

Fish Batter

1 cup self-rising flour
3 tablespoons self-rising cornmeal
1 teaspoon sugar
3 teaspoons salt
Black pepper
1 cup cool water
1 egg, slightly beaten
1 tablespoon oil

- In a mixing bowl, combine the flour, cornmeal, sugar, salt, and plenty of pepper.
- In a separate bowl or measuring cup, combine the water, egg, and oil.
- Combine the dry ingredients with the liquids; mix well.

Note: Great for crappie or bass fillets, which should be well-drained on paper toweling in order for batter to stick.

Sauces

B. McWilliams

Basic Barbeque Sauce

2 tablespoons vegetable oil
1 onion, finely chopped
3 cloves garlic, minced
1½ cups ketchup or
  tomato sauce
½ cup cider vinegar
¼ cup Worcestershire
  sauce
⅓ cup sugar
1 tablespoon chili powder
½ teaspoon ground red
  pepper, more or less

• Heat oil in saucepan over moderate heat; add onion and garlic. Cook gently, stirring frequently, for 5 minutes. Add ketchup, vinegar, Worcestershire sauce, sugar, chili powder, and red pepper to taste.

• Reduce heat and simmer, partially covered, until sauce has thickened slightly, about 20 minutes.

Yield: 2½ cups

Meat Marinade

2 eggs, beaten
1 5-ounce can evaporated
  milk
1 tablespoon baking
  powder
2 tablespoons vinegar
Creole seasoning
Flour

• Combine eggs, evaporated milk, baking powder, and vinegar, mixing well. Marinate dove, duck, shrimp, venison, or beef at least 1 hour.

• Remove meat; discard marinade. Season with Creole seasoning; dredge in flour before frying.

Yield: 1 cup

Dry Marinades

For Lamb, Beef, and Chicken

2 tablespoons chopped fresh
rosemary or 2 teaspoons
dried rosemary
2 large cloves garlic, minced
1½ teaspoons salt
1 teaspoon freshly ground
black pepper
Freshly grated zest of
1 lemon or lime

For Fish

2 tablespoons chopped fresh
dill or 2 teaspoons dried
dill
2 teaspoons mild paprika
1 tablespoon grated lemon
zest
1 teaspoon salt
1 teaspoon freshly ground
black pepper
¼ teaspoon ground red
pepper

For Pork

2 tablespoons chopped fresh
thyme or 2 teaspoons dried
thyme
1 tablespoon chopped fresh
sage or 1 teaspoon dried
sage
2 teaspoons salt
1 teaspoon freshly ground
black pepper
¼ teaspoon ground allspice
or cloves
2 cloves garlic, minced

• Select list of ingredients that
complements the food you are
marinating. Combine ingredients in a small bowl, stirring
to mix.

*Note: Rub meat, poultry, or fish
lightly with oil before coating
with marinade. Made with fresh
herbs, these marinades will
keep if refrigerated, tightly
covered, up to 3 days. Made
with dried herbs, mixture will
keep for several weeks stored in
airtight container in cupboard.*

257

Steak or Shish Kabob Marinade

1 cup vegetable oil
¾ cup soy sauce
½ cup lemon juice
¼ cup Worcestershire sauce
¼ cup prepared mustard
1 to 2 teaspoons black
   pepper
2 cloves garlic, minced

• Combine all ingredients in container, stirring to mix thoroughly.

• Marinate meat for 4 to 8 hours.

Yield: 2¾ cups

Hollandaise Sauce

½ pound (2 sticks) butter,
   divided
3 egg yolks
1 tablespoon cold water
1 tablespoon lemon juice
Dash of salt
White pepper

• Melt ¾ cup of the butter; set aside.

• Beat egg yolks until thick. Place yolks in top of double boiler; add water, lemon juice, and salt. Beat well; place over simmering water. Add 1 tablespoon of the remaining butter; stir with wire whisk until thick enough to see bottom of pan between strokes, about 5 minutes.

• Remove pan from hot water; beat in remaining 3 table-spoons of the butter. Pour melted butter into mixture, very slowly, beating con-stantly. (If sauce curdles, beat in 1 tablespoon cold water.) Stir in white pepper.

Yield: 1 cup

Note: Will keep in refrigerator several days or will freeze well. Thaw sauce and allow to reach room temperature.

Steak Sauce

⅓ cup butter
⅓ cup Worcestershire
  sauce
½ lemon, juiced
1 teaspoon prepared
  mustard
⅓ cup steak sauce
2 cups sliced mushrooms

- In a saucepan, melt butter over low heat; add Worcestershire sauce and lemon juice, stirring until blended.
- In a small bowl, combine mustard and steak sauce; mix until smooth. Stir into butter mixture.
- Cover and cook 5 to 8 minutes. Add mushrooms; simmer 5 additional minutes.

Yield: 3 cups

Mushroom-Garlic Sauce for Steak

1 cup water
1 tablespoon all-purpose
  flour
1 lemon, juiced
¼ cup Worcestershire
  sauce
1 garlic clove, crushed
1 4-ounce jar mushrooms
¼ pound (1 stick) butter
Salt
Pepper

- Combine water, flour, lemon juice, and Worcestershire sauce, mixing thoroughly. Set aside.
- Sauté garlic and mushrooms in butter. Add water mixture. Stir in salt and pepper to taste.

Yield: 2½ cups

White Sauce

Thin White Sauce

1 tablespoon butter
1 tablespoon all-purpose
flour
1 cup milk
¼ teaspoon salt
Dash of white pepper

Medium White Sauce

2 tablespoons butter
2 tablespoons all-purpose
flour
1 cup milk
¼ teaspoon salt
Dash of white pepper

Thick White Sauce

3 tablespoons butter
3 tablespoons all-purpose
flour
1 cup milk
¼ teaspoon salt
Dash of white pepper

• Melt butter in heavy saucepan over low heat; add flour, stirring until smooth. Cook 1 minute, stirring constantly.

• Gradually add milk; cook over medium heat, stirring constantly, until thickened and bubbly. Stir in salt and pepper. Serve over poached eggs, poultry, seafood, or vegetables.

Yield: 1 cup

Dill Sauce for Lamb

3 tablespoons butter
1 tablespoon all-purpose
   flour
1 cup chicken broth
¼ cup chopped chives
1¼ teaspoons dill weed
¼ cup finely chopped
   parsley
1½ teaspoons lemon juice

- Heat butter in saucepan; blend in flour and cook until bubbly. Remove from heat; add chicken broth slowly, stirring constantly. Cook until thickened, about 3 minutes.
- Stir in remaining ingredients; keep warm to serve. Store leftover sauce in refrigerator.

Yield: 1½ cups

Horseradish Sauce

1 16-ounce carton sour
   cream
1 5-ounce jar horseradish
2 cups mayonnaise
Salt
White pepper

- Combine sour cream, horseradish, and mayonnaise, mixing well. Season with salt and pepper to taste.

Yield: 4½ cups

Note: Serve over any red meat or on sandwiches, such as roast beef or ham.

Basting Sauce

3 quarts vinegar
1½ cups salt
8 tablespoons pepper
8 tablespoons chili powder
4 tablespoons sugar

- Combine all ingredients in a stock pot or Dutch oven; heat until sugar dissolves, stirring occasionally. Cool. Store in airtight container.

Yield: 3 quarts

Note: Will keep unrefrigerated indefinitely. Use to baste beef, game, seafood, or poultry on the grill.

261

Sweet and Sour Sauce

6 to 8 maraschino cherries plus 2 tablespoons juice
1 8-ounce can chunk pineapple plus ½ cup juice
1½ tablespoons cornstarch
1 tablespoon soy sauce
1 tablespoon vinegar
1 tablespoon brown sugar
2 tablespoons ketchup
½ cup pineapple juice

• Combine all ingredients in bowl of blender or food processor; process until well mixed. Heat until thickened, stirring constantly. (More pineapple juice can be added to thin.) Refrigerate.

Yield: 2 cups

Note: Serve with egg rolls or any Chinese dish.

Hot Chocolate Sauce

¼ pound (1 stick) butter
3 1-ounce semisweet chocolate squares
1 cup sugar
4 ounces evaporated milk

• Combine butter and chocolate in top of double boiler over simmering water; cook until melted, stirring frequently. Stir in sugar and milk. Remove top pan; place over low direct heat. Cook until sugar is dissolved.

• Bring to a rapid boil for 8 minutes, stirring constantly.

Yield: 12 servings

Note: Serve over brownies and ice cream. Can reheat in microwave if desired.

Curry Sauce

2 tablespoons butter
3 tablespoons minced
   onion
1½ teaspoons curry
   powder
¾ teaspoon sugar
⅛ teaspoon ground ginger
2 tablespoons all-purpose
   flour
1 cup milk
⅛ teaspoon salt
Dash of white pepper
1 teaspoon lemon juice

• Melt butter in heavy saucepan over low heat. Add minced onion, curry powder, sugar, and ground ginger; sauté until onion is tender. Add flour, stirring until smooth. Cook 1 minute, stirring constantly.

• Gradually add milk; cook over medium heat, stirring constantly, until thickened and bubbly. Stir in salt, pepper, and lemon juice.

Yield: 1¼ cups

Note: Serve over poached eggs, poultry, or vegetables.

Tomato Sauce

6 tablespoons olive oil
1 medium onion, thinly
   sliced
3 cloves garlic, crushed
3 cups ripe tomatoes,
   peeled, cored, seeded,
   and finely chopped
2 tablespoons chopped
   fresh basil
1 teaspoon salt
1 teaspoon pepper
1 teaspoon sugar
½ cup tomato paste

• Heat oil in skillet over medium heat; stir in onion, garlic, tomatoes, and basil. Cook, stirring occasionally, until vegetables are tender. Season with salt, pepper, and sugar, stirring to blend. Add tomato paste. Simmer.

Yield: 4½ cups

Sauce for Artichokes

¼ cup lemon juice
½ cup firmly packed fresh
 basil
½ teaspoon salt
1 clove garlic, minced
¼ cup chopped parsley
1 cup mayonnaise

• Combine lemon juice, basil, salt, garlic, and parsley, mixing well. Fold in mayonnaise. Refrigerate.

Yield: 2 cups

Artichokes

6 artichokes, stems and
 outer tough leaves
 removed
½ lemon, juiced
2 to 3 cloves garlic,
 chopped
6 to 8 cloves
1 teaspoon salt
1 tablespoon vegetable or
 olive oil

• Combine all ingredients in Dutch oven with enough water to cover. Bring to a boil; reduce heat, and simmer 22 minutes, or until tender. Drain and serve with sauce.

Yield: 6 servings

Homemade Mayonnaise

2 egg yolks
1 whole egg
1 tablespoon prepared
 Dijon mustard
Pinch of salt
Freshly ground black
 pepper
¼ cup fresh lemon juice,
 divided
2 cups vegetable oil

- Combine egg yolks, whole egg, mustard, salt and pepper to taste, and half of the lemon juice in bowl of food processor. Process 1 minute.

- While motor is running, pour in oil very slowly in a steady stream. (This will take a little time.) Shut off motor and scrape down sides of bowl with rubber spatula. Replace top; turn on processor. Add remaining lemon juice; process few seconds. Add more lemon juice if mayonnaise is too thick.

- Pour into covered jar and refrigerate. Will keep refrigerated 2 to 3 weeks.

Yield: 3 cups

Herbed Mayonnaise

1 cup homemade mayonnaise
 (or commercially-prepared
 mayonnaise)
1 cup fresh watercress
 leaves, rinsed and blotted
 dry
¼ cup fresh chopped Italian
 or curly parsley
¼ cup fresh snipped chives

- Combine all ingredients in bowl of food processor. Process until smooth; don't overprocess.

Yield: 1 cup

265

Lite Blender Mayonnaise

⅓ cup egg substitute
½ teaspoon dry mustard,
    optional
¼ teaspoon salt
¼ teaspoon paprika
1 cup vegetable oil, divided
3 tablespoons lemon juice
    or 2 tablespoons white
    vinegar

• Combine egg substitute,
  mustard if desired, salt,
  paprika, and ½ cup of the oil
  in bowl of blender. Process
  on medium-high speed until
  barely mixed.

• Pour in the remaining ½ cup
  oil in slow, steady stream with
  blender running. Add lemon
  juice. Add more salt and
  lemon juice, if needed. Will
  keep refrigerated 2 weeks.

Yield: 1½ cups

Homemade Mustard

1 4-ounce can dry mustard
1 cup white vinegar
1 cup sugar
2 egg yolks, beaten
¾ cup prepared mustard
1½ cups mayonnaise-type
    salad dressing

• Combine dry mustard and
  vinegar. Cover; let stand
  overnight.

• In a double boiler, combine
  mustard and vinegar mixture,
  sugar, and beaten egg yolks.
  Cook over medium heat until
  thickened, stirring occasionally. While hot, add prepared
  mustard. Remove from heat,
  and add mayonnaise-type
  salad dressing.

Yield: 3½ cups

Eggplant and Basil Pizza Sauce

2 small eggplant, peeled
  and diced into 1-inch
  cubes
Salt
1 15-ounce can diced
  tomatoes or 3 fresh
  tomatoes, peeled and
  diced
1 8-ounce can tomato
  sauce
2 to 3 tablespoons dried
  basil
1½ teaspoons dry Italian
  seasoning

- Boil eggplant in salted water until tender; drain. Mash in bowl. Set aside.
- Simmer tomatoes 5 to 10 minutes. Add tomato sauce, eggplant, basil, and Italian seasoning. Simmer 10 to 15 minutes.

Yield: 3½ cups

Note: Rub commercially-prepared pizza crust with small amount of olive oil; top with Eggplant and Basil Pizza Sauce and toppings, such as sliced onions, bell pepper, and sautéed mushrooms. Bake according to directions on pizza crust.

Apple-Mustard Glaze for Ham

1 cup apple jelly
1 tablespoon prepared
  mustard
1 tablespoon lemon juice
¼ teaspoon ground
  nutmeg

- In small saucepan, combine all ingredients; bring to a boil, stirring constantly. Remove from heat. Use to baste ham during last 30 minutes of baking.

Yield: 1 cup

267

Raisin Sauce for Ham

½ cup raisins
1½ cups water
1 lemon, juiced
1 orange, juiced
¼ teaspoon cinnamon
¼ teaspoon ground cloves
½ cup sugar
2 teaspoons cornstarch
1 tablespoon butter

• Combine raisins and water in small saucepan; soak 30 minutes. Simmer over medium heat 15 minutes. Add lemon juice, orange juice, cinnamon, and cloves.
• Mix sugar and cornstarch in small bowl. Add enough water to dissolve. Gradually stir mixture into raisins. Cook over medium heat until thickened, stirring constantly. (Mixture will continue to thicken after being removed from heat.)
• Stir in butter until barely melted.

Yield: 2 cups

Note: Serve with sliced ham.

Raspberry Sauce

1 12-ounce package frozen unsweetened raspberries, thawed
6 tablespoons sugar
2 tablespoons raspberry liqueur

• Combine raspberries and sugar in small saucepan; bring to a boil and cook until sugar dissolves. Stir in liqueur.

Yield: 2 cups

Note: Serve with pound cake, ice cream, or sliced ham.

Desserts

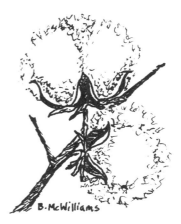

B. McWilliams

Amaretto Cake

½ pound (2 sticks) butter, softened
2½ cups sugar
6 eggs, room temperature
1 cup sour cream, room temperature
1 teaspoon vanilla extract
1 teaspoon orange extract
1 teaspoon lemon extract
2 teaspoons almond extract
¼ teaspoon baking soda
½ teaspoon salt
3 cups cake flour, sifted 3 times and measured
½ cup amaretto liqueur
Glaze
1 cup chopped almonds, lightly toasted

- Preheat oven to 325 degrees.
- Combine butter and sugar; cream together until light and fluffy. Add eggs one at a time, beating well after each addition. Add sour cream; beat until blended. Stir in extracts, baking soda, and salt. Gradually add cake flour and beat well. Add liqueur. Pour into large greased Bundt cake pan.
- Bake 1 hour and 15 minutes, or until a wooden pick inserted in center of cake comes out clean. Turn out onto wire rack; cool.
- Drizzle Glaze on cooled cake; sprinkle with almonds.

Yield: 12 servings

Glaze

1 8-ounce jar orange marmalade
4 ounces apricot preserves
¼ cup amaretto liqueur

- Combine all ingredients in a saucepan; heat over medium heat until marmalade and preserves are dissolved, stirring often.

Fresh Apple Cake

1¼ cups vegetable oil
2 cups sugar
3 cups all-purpose flour
1 teaspoon baking soda
1 teaspoon salt
3 eggs, slightly beaten
2 teaspoons vanilla extract
3 cups peeled and chopped
apple
1 cup chopped nuts

- Preheat oven to 325 degrees.
- In a large mixing bowl, combine oil and sugar, beating until light and fluffy.
- Sift together the flour, baking soda, and salt; add to sugar mixture. Beat until blended. Stir in eggs. Add vanilla. Fold in apples and nuts. Pour into a greased and floured tube or Bundt pan.
- Bake 1½ hours, or until a wooden pick inserted in center of cake comes out clean. Cool on wire rack. Invert onto serving plate. Top with Brown Sugar Glaze.

Yield: 12 servings

Brown Sugar Glaze

1 cup firmly packed brown
sugar
¼ pound (1 stick) butter
¼ cup evaporated milk
1 teaspoon vanilla extract

- Combine all ingredients in a saucepan; bring to full boil, stirring often. Remove from heat. Cool slightly.
- Pour into a mixing bowl; beat until cooled and thickened.

Apricot Nectar Cake

1 18½-ounce package
  yellow deluxe cake mix
4 eggs, separated
¾ cup vegetable oil
¾ cup apricot nectar
Icing

- Preheat oven to 325 degrees.
- Combine cake mix, egg yolks, oil, and apricot nectar; mix until well blended. Fold in beaten egg whites. Pour into greased and floured tube pan.
- Bake 55 minutes, or until wooden pick inserted in center of cake comes out clean. Cool on wire rack. Invert onto serving plate. Pour Icing over top and sides of cake.

Yield: 12 servings

Icing

2 cups confectioners'
  sugar
¾ cup apricot nectar
½ lemon, juiced

- Combine all ingredients, beating until smooth.

Blueberry Cake

3 eggs
1 8-ounce package cream
  cheese, softened
½ cup vegetable oil
1 18½-ounce package
  butter cake mix
1 15-ounce can
  blueberries, drained

- Preheat oven to 350 degrees.
- Combine eggs, cream cheese, and oil in large mixing bowl; beat by hand until well blended. Add cake mix; beat by hand until mixed. Fold in blueberries. Pour into greased Bundt or tube pan.
- Bake 40 minutes, or until wooden pick inserted in center of cake comes out clean.

Yield: 12 servings

Carrot Cake

2 cups all-purpose flour
2 cups sugar
2 teaspoons baking soda
1 teaspoon baking powder
½ teaspoon salt
1 teaspoon cinnamon
2 4-ounce jars carrot baby food or 3 cups grated carrot (see Note)
4 eggs, well beaten
1½ cups vegetable oil
1 teaspoon vanilla extract
Cream Cheese Frosting

• Preheat oven to 350 degrees.
• Combine flour, sugar, baking soda, baking powder, salt, and cinnamon in a large mixing bowl, stirring until blended. Add carrot, eggs, oil, and vanilla; beat until mixed. Pour into 3 greased and floured 9-inch cake pans.
• Bake 30 minutes, or until wooden pick inserted in center of cake comes out clean. Spread Cream Cheese Frosting between layers and on top of cake while still warm.

Yield: 12 servings

Note: Carrot baby food makes for a very moist and delicious cake—plus it's much easier!

Cream Cheese Frosting

1 16-ounce package confectioners' sugar
1 8-ounce package cream cheese, softened
¼ pound (1 stick) butter, softened
1 teaspoon vanilla extract
1 cup chopped pecans

• Combine sugar, cream cheese, butter, and vanilla in a mixing bowl. Beat until smooth and creamy. Fold in pecans.

Cheesecake with Sour Cream Topping

Crust

1⅔ cups graham cracker crumbs
2 tablespoons sugar
1 teaspoon cinnamon
6 tablespoons butter, melted

Filling

2 8-ounce packages cream cheese, softened
⅔ cup sugar
2 eggs, well beaten
½ teaspoon vanilla extract

Sour Cream Topping

1 8-ounce carton sour cream
¼ teaspoon vanilla extract
2 tablespoons sugar

- Preheat oven to 375 degrees.
- To prepare Crust, combine crumbs, sugar, cinnamon, and butter in a small bowl; stir until blended. Press into bottom of 9 by 13-inch baking dish. Set aside.
- To prepare Filling, combine cream cheese, sugar, eggs, and vanilla in a large mixing bowl. Beat until mixture is smooth and creamy. Pour into prepared crust.
- Bake 15 to 20 minutes; cool. Increase oven temperature to 500 degrees.
- To prepare Sour Cream Topping, combine sour cream, vanilla, and sugar in a small bowl; beat until well mixed. Spoon over cooled cheesecake. Bake an additional 5 minutes.

Yield: 12 servings

Never Fail Cheesecake

Crust

20 graham cracker squares, crushed
1 tablespoon sugar
1 tablespoon butter, melted

Filling

3 8-ounce packages cream cheese, softened
5 eggs
1½ cups sugar, divided
2½ teaspoons vanilla extract, divided
2 tablespoons all-purpose flour
½ teaspoon baking powder
1 16-ounce container sour cream
Fruit pie filling, optional

• Preheat oven to 300 degrees.

• To prepare Crust, combine crumbs, sugar, and butter, stirring until blended. Press into bottom of 10-inch springform pan. Set aside.

• To prepare Filling, beat cream cheese in a mixing bowl until soft. Add eggs one at a time, beating well after each addition. Add 1 cup of the sugar and 1½ teaspoons of the vanilla, mixing well. Stir in flour and baking powder. Slowly pour over prepared crust.

• Bake 1 hour and 10 minutes, or until knife inserted in center comes out clean. Do not turn off oven.

• Mix sour cream with the remaining ½ cup sugar and the remaining 1 teaspoon vanilla; pour slowly over cheesecake. Return to oven and bake 5 additional minutes. Cool to room temperature. Chill. Serve topped with pie filling, if desired.

Yield: one 10-inch cheesecake
(10 to 12 servings)

Chocolate Sheet Cake

2 cups sugar
2 cups all-purpose flour
3 tablespoons cocoa
¼ pound (1 stick) butter
1 cup water
½ cup vegetable oil
½ cup buttermilk
1 teaspoon baking soda
2 eggs, unbeaten
1 teaspoon vanilla extract

• Preheat oven to 400 degrees.
• In a mixing bowl, combine sugar, flour, and cocoa; mix until blended.
• In a saucepan, combine butter, water, and oil. Cook over low heat until butter is dissolved, stirring occasionally. Pour butter mixture into dry ingredients. Beat until mixed. Cool.
• In a separate large mixing bowl, combine buttermilk, baking soda, eggs, and vanilla. Stir in chocolate mixture. Pour into greased and floured 9 by 13-inch baking pan.
• Bake 30 minutes, or until wooden pick inserted in center of cake comes out clean. Top with Chocolate Icing while cake is still in pan and hot.

Yield: 10 to 12 servings

Chocolate Icing

4 tablespoons cocoa
¼ pound (1 stick) butter
6 tablespoons buttermilk
1 16-ounce box
  confectioners' sugar
1 teaspoon vanilla extract
1 cup chopped nuts, optional

• Combine cocoa, butter, and buttermilk in a saucepan. Bring to a boil. Combine confectioners sugar and chocolate mixture in a mixing bowl, beating well. Stir in vanilla and nuts.

Coconut Cake

½ pound (2 sticks) butter, softened
2½ cups sugar
5 egg yolks, reserving whites for Boiled Frosting
2½ cups self-rising flour (may use up to 3 cups)
1½ cups milk
1 teaspoon salt
1½ teaspoons vanilla extract
1 cup coconut, plus extra for garnish

- Preheat oven to 300 degrees.
- In a large mixing bowl, cream butter and sugar until light and fluffy. Add egg yolks one at a time, beating well after each addition. Add flour, milk, salt, and vanilla, mixing just until dry ingredients are moistened. Stir in coconut. Pour into 3 greased and floured 9-inch cake pans.
- Bake 30 minutes, or until wooden pick inserted in center comes out clean. Cool on wire racks. Frost with Boiled Frosting, spreading between layers and on top and sides of cake. Sprinkle with additional coconut.

Yield: 8 to 12 servings

Boiled Frosting

1½ cups sugar
⅓ cup corn syrup, optional
½ cup water
5 egg whites
1 teaspoon vanilla extract

- In a heavy saucepan, combine sugar, corn syrup, and water. Boil until mixture reaches 240 degrees on a candy thermometer, or until mixture spins a thread from a metal spoon. (Do not stir, or mixture will be sugary.)
- In a mixing bowl, beat egg whites until mixture stands in peaks. Slowly pour hot mixture in a thin stream into egg whites, beating constantly. Beat until frosting is stiff enough to spread. Stir in vanilla.

Cranberry Cake

2 cups all-purpose flour, plus 3 additional teaspoons for dusting cranberries
1 cup sugar
2 teaspoons baking powder
½ teaspoon salt
1 cup milk
3 tablespoons butter, melted
2 cups fresh cranberries, washed and drained

- Preheat oven to 350 degrees.
- Sift together 2 cups of the flour, sugar, baking powder, and salt in a large mixing bowl. Stir in milk and butter, mixing well.
- Dust cranberries with the remaining 3 teaspoons flour. Gently stir into flour mixture. Pour into a greased 9 by 13-inch baking dish.
- Bake 25 to 30 minutes; do not brown. Cake should be very moist. Cut into squares; spoon Cream Sauce over each serving.

Yield: 10 to 12 servings

Cream Sauce

¼ pound (1 stick) butter
1 cup sugar
¾ cup whipping cream

- Combine all ingredients in a saucepan; bring to a boil, stirring to melt sugar. Serve warm.

Pear Cake with Caramel Drizzle

3 eggs, beaten
1¾ cups sugar
1 cup vegetable oil
1 tablespoon vanilla
  extract
1½ cups all-purpose flour
1 cup whole wheat flour
2 teaspoons baking
  powder
1 teaspoon baking soda
1 teaspoon allspice
3 cups peeled, chopped
  pears (about 4 medium)
1 cup chopped pecans
Caramel Drizzle

• Preheat oven to 375 degrees.
• Combine eggs, sugar, and oil in a large bowl; beat at medium speed. Add vanilla.
• Combine flours, baking powder, baking soda, and allspice; add to sugar mixture alternately with pears. Stir in pecans. Pour into well-greased and floured Bundt pan.
• Bake 55 minutes, or until wooden pick inserted in center comes out clean. Cool in pan 10 minutes; remove from pan and cool completely on wire rack. Spoon Caramel Drizzle over cake.

Yield: 8 to 12 servings

Caramel Drizzle

4 tablespoons butter
¼ cup firmly packed dark
  brown sugar
2 tablespoons milk
1 cup sifted confectioners'
  sugar
½ teaspoon vanilla extract
Pinch of salt

• Melt butter in a saucepan; cook over medium heat until light brown, stirring constantly. Add brown sugar, and cook until sugar melts. Remove from heat.
• Pour brown sugar mixture into a mixing bowl; add milk, stirring constantly. Slowly add confectioners' sugar, vanilla, and salt, beating at medium speed. Beat until mixture reaches glaze consistency.

Yield: 1⅓ cups

Pound Cake

½ pound (2 sticks) butter,
  softened
2 cups sugar
4 large or 5 small eggs,
  separated
1 cup milk
3 cups self-rising flour
1 teaspoon vanilla extract
1 teaspoon almond extract

- Preheat oven to 325 degrees.
- In a mixing bowl, cream butter and sugar until light and fluffy. Add egg yolks, beating well. Alternately add milk and flour, beating well after each addition.
- In a separate small bowl, beat egg whites until stiff peaks form. Fold into flour mixture; add vanilla and almond extracts. Pour into greased Bundt or tube pan.
- Bake 1 hour and 15 minutes, or until lightly browned. Cool in pan 10 minutes; remove from pan and cool completely on wire rack.

Yield: 8 to 12 servings

Sour Cream Cake

1 18½-ounce package
    yellow cake mix
1 8-ounce container sour
    cream
½ cup vegetable oil
¼ cup sugar
4 eggs

Filling

2 tablespoons firmly
    packed brown sugar
1 teaspoon cinnamon
1 cup chopped pecans

- Preheat oven to 350 degrees.
- In a large mixing bowl, combine cake mix, sour cream, oil, and sugar, beating well. Add eggs one at a time, mixing well after each addition. Pour ½ of the batter into a greased tube pan.
- To prepare Filling, combine brown sugar, cinnamon, and pecans, mixing well.
- Sprinkle Filling over batter in pan. Add remaining batter and swirl with knife.
- Bake 50 minutes, or until lightly browned. Cool in pan 15 minutes; invert onto serving plate. Drizzle with Lemon Glaze.

Yield: 8 to 12 servings

Lemon Glaze

1⅓ cups confectioners'
    sugar
2 tablespoons lemon juice

- Combine both ingredients in small bowl, mixing until smooth.

Red Velvet Cake

½ cup shortening
1½ cups sugar
2 eggs
2 ounces red food coloring
2 tablespoons cocoa
1 scant teaspoon salt
2¼ cups all-purpose flour
1 cup buttermilk
1 teaspoon vanilla extract
1 teaspoon butter flavoring
1 teaspoon baking soda
1 tablespoon vinegar
Chopped nuts or coconut
   for garnish, optional

- Preheat oven to 350 degrees.
- Cream shortening and sugar until light and fluffy. Add eggs, beating well.
- In a small bowl, combine food coloring and cocoa; stir to make a paste. Add to creamed mixture. Stir in salt, flour, buttermilk, vanilla, and butter flavoring; beat until blended. Add soda and vinegar; do not beat hard, just blend. Pour into 2 greased and floured 9-inch cake pans.
- Bake 30 minutes, or until wooden pick inserted in center of cake comes out clean.Cool 10 minutes in pan. Invert onto wire racks; cool completely. Frost between layers and on top and sides of cake with Frosting. Garnish with nuts or coconut, if desired. Refrigerate.

Yield: 8 to 12 servings

Frosting

3 tablespoons all-purpose
   flour
1 cup milk
½ pound (2 sticks) butter,
   softened
1 cup sugar
1 teaspoon vanilla extract

- Combine flour and milk in a saucepan; cook over low heat until thickened.
- In a mixing bowl, cream butter, sugar, and vanilla until light and fluffy. Slowly add milk mixture, beating constantly. Continue beating until frosting is creamy and soft peaks form.

Strawberry Cake

1 18½-ounce package
  white cake mix
1 cup vegetable oil
4 eggs
¼ cup water
1 3-ounce package
  strawberry Jell-o
Juice from 10-ounce
  package frozen
  strawberries, thawed
  (reserve berries for icing)

• Preheat oven to 350 degrees.
• In a mixing bowl, combine
  cake mix and oil, mixing until
  blended. Add eggs one at a
  time, beating well after each
  addition. Stir in water, Jell-o,
  and juice from strawberries;
  beat. Pour into greased and
  floured Bundt pan.
• Bake 45 minutes to 1 hour,
  or until wooden pick inserted
  in center comes out clean.
  Cool 20 minutes in pan.
  Invert onto wire rack; cool
  completely. Pour Strawberry
  Icing over top and sides of
  cake.

Yield: 8 to 12 servings

Strawberry Icing

1 16-ounce package
  confectioners' sugar
¾ cup (1½ sticks) butter,
  melted
Reserved strawberries
  from 10-ounce package
  frozen strawberries,
  thawed

• Combine sugar and butter in
  a mixing bowl. Pour in
  strawberries; stir until
  blended.

Piña Colada Cake

1 18½-ounce package white or yellow cake mix with pudding
1 14-ounce can sweetened condensed milk
1 8-ounce can cream of coconut
1 20-ounce can crushed pineapple, drained
1 16-ounce container frozen whipped topping, thawed
1 6-ounce package frozen coconut, thawed
Chopped pecans, optional
Chopped cherries, optional

- Bake cake according to package directions for a 9 by 13-inch cake.
- While cake is baking, combine condensed milk, cream of coconut, and pineapple, mixing well.
- Make small holes in warm cake; pour pineapple mixture on top. Cool.
- Frost with whipped topping; cover top with coconut. Garnish with chopped pecans and cherries, if desired.

Yield: 9 to 12 servings

Microwave Pralines

1 16-ounce box light brown sugar
1 cup whipping cream
2 tablespoons butter
1 teaspoon vanilla extract
2 cups broken pecans

- Combine brown sugar and whipping cream in 2-quart bowl. Microwave on HI 12 to 14 minutes, or until mixture reaches soft ball stage (234 degrees). Stir once during cooking.
- Stir in remaining ingredients. Cook an additional 1 to 2 minutes on HI, or until soft ball stage is again reached. Working quickly, drop by teaspoonfuls onto greased wax paper.

Yield: 2 dozen

Dipped Candy

¼ pound (1 stick) butter, softened
1 14-ounce can sweetened condensed milk
1 teaspoon vanilla extract
1 16-ounce box confectioners' sugar, sifted
1 3½-ounce can coconut
1 cup finely chopped nuts
1 6-ounce bag chocolate chips
⅓ block paraffin

- Cream butter until light and fluffy. Stir in milk and vanilla. Gradually add sugar, mixing well. Fold in coconut and nuts until blended. Chill.
- Meanwhile, melt chocolate and paraffin in top of double boiler over simmering water.
- Roll chilled mixture into very small balls; dip in melted chocolate mixture using a long-handled slotted spoon. (Leave only long enough to coat evenly with chocolate.) Place on wax paper to cool.

Yield: 4 dozen

Chocolate Fudge

2 cups sugar
⅔ cup evaporated milk
12 large marshmallows
¼ pound (1 stick) butter
Pinch of salt
1 6-ounce package semisweet chocolate chips
1 cup chopped pecans
1 teaspoon vanilla extract

- In a heavy 2-quart saucepan, combine sugar, milk, marshmallows, butter, and salt. Cook, stirring constantly, over medium heat to boiling. Boil and stir 5 minutes. Remove from heat.
- Stir in chocolate chips until completely melted. Stir in nuts and vanilla. Spread in greased 8 by 8-inch pan; cool. Cut into pieces.

Yield: Approximately 25 pieces

Honeydew Candy

3 cups sugar
1 12-ounce can
  evaporated milk
¼ pound (1 stick) butter
½ cup corn syrup
2 cups chopped pecans

- Combine sugar, milk, butter, and corn syrup in a heavy saucepan; cook until mixture reaches 234 degrees on a candy thermometer, or until mixture forms a soft ball when dropped in cold water. Stir in pecans. Remove from heat.
- Beat mixture until cooled and thickened. Drop by teaspoonfuls onto wax paper.

Yield: 3 dozen

Millionaires

1 14-ounce package
  caramels
2 tablespoons evaporated
  milk or cream
2 cups broken pecans
1 cup chocolate chips
⅓ block paraffin

- Combine caramels and milk in top of double boiler over simmering water; heat until caramels are melted, stirring occasionally. Add pecans, mixing well. Drop by teaspoonfuls onto greased baking sheet. Cool in refrigerator for at least 1 hour.
- Combine chocolate chips and paraffin in top of double boiler, stirring until melted. Remove from heat. Dip caramel and pecan pieces into chocolate mixture. Cool on wax paper.

Yield: 2 dozen

Almond Sugar Cookies

½ pound (2 sticks)
   unsalted butter, softened
1½ cups sugar
2 eggs
3 teaspoons vanilla extract
3 cups all-purpose flour
1 teaspoon baking powder
¼ teaspoon salt
Almond Icing

- In a mixing bowl, cream butter; add sugar and beat until light and fluffy. Stir in eggs one at a time, mixing well after each addition. Add vanilla, beating until blended.
- Sift together the flour, baking powder, and salt. Add to creamed mixture, mixing until well blended. Wrap in plastic wrap and refrigerate at least 4 hours or overnight.
- Preheat oven to 350 degrees.
- Roll out dough on generously floured surface to ¼-inch thickness; cut with cookie cutter. Transfer to greased cookie sheet with turner. (May also use cookie press.) Bake 12 to 15 minutes. Cool on wire racks. Frost with Almond Icing.

Yield: 4 dozen

Almond Icing

4 tablespoons butter,
   softened
1 16-ounce box
   confectioners' sugar
1 tablespoon almond
   extract
Milk

- Combine butter and confectioners' sugar, mixing well. Stir in almond extract. Add 1 tablespoon milk at a time until desired consistency is reached.

Cocoons

½ pound (2 sticks) butter, softened
1 teaspoon vanilla extract
2½ cups all-purpose flour
7 tablespoons sugar
½ teaspoon salt
2 cups chopped nuts
Confectioners' sugar

- Preheat oven to 350 degrees.
- Melt butter in a small saucepan over low heat; stir in vanilla. Cool.
- In a mixing bowl, combine the butter mixture, flour, sugar, salt, and nuts. Shape into very small finger-shaped cookies; place on ungreased cookie sheet.
- Bake 25 minutes. Roll in confectioners' sugar while still warm.

Yield: 4 to 5 dozen

Note: Nice for teas and receptions. Will keep in cookie tin for a week or more.

Lace Cookies

2 cups regular oats, uncooked
2 tablespoons all-purpose flour
1½ cups sugar
½ pound (2 sticks) butter, melted
½ teaspoon salt
2 teaspoons baking powder
2 eggs, beaten
3 teaspoons vanilla extract
1½ cups pecans

- Preheat oven to 325 degrees.
- Combine oats, flour, sugar, butter, salt, baking powder, eggs, and vanilla, mixing well. Stir in pecans. Drop by rounded spoonfuls onto foil-lined greased cookie sheet.
- Bake 10 to 15 minutes. Cool on wire racks.

Yield: 3 dozen

Macadamia White Chocolate Cookies

2¼ cups all-purpose flour
1 teaspoon baking soda
¼ teaspoon salt
½ pound (2 sticks) butter, softened
¾ cup sugar
⅔ cup firmly packed brown sugar
1 teaspoon vanilla extract
2 eggs
1 12-ounce package white chocolate chips
1 3½-ounce jar macadamia nuts, coarsely chopped

• Preheat oven to 350 degrees.
• Sift together flour, baking soda, and salt; set aside.
• In a large mixing bowl, combine butter, sugars, and vanilla, beating until creamy. Stir in eggs until well blended. Gradually add flour mixture. Stir in chips and nuts. Drop by rounded spoonfuls onto lightly greased cookie sheet.
• Bake 9 to 11 minutes, or until golden. Remove from pan; cool on wire racks.

Yield: 4 dozen

Chocolate Oatmeal Cookies

¼ pound (1 stick) butter
2 cups sugar
2 tablespoons cocoa
Pinch of salt
½ cup milk
½ cup peanut butter
2½ cups oats

• Combine butter, sugar, cocoa, salt, and milk in a saucepan. Bring to a boil; boil 1 minute, stirring constantly.
• Remove from heat.
• Stir in peanut butter, mixing well. Add oats; stir to combine. Drop by teaspoonfuls onto wax paper. Cool.

Yield: 3 dozen

Banana Pudding

2 cups milk
2 eggs, separated
⅔ cup plus ¼ cup sugar,
divided
⅛ teaspoon salt
2 tablespoons cornstarch
1½ teaspoons vanilla
extract
48 vanilla wafers
4 or 5 ripe bananas, sliced

- Pour milk in top of double boiler over boiling water; heat until scalded.
- Beat egg yolks. Add ⅔ cup sugar, salt, and cornstarch. Blend about ½ cup scalded milk into egg mixture. Add egg mixture to remaining milk in double boiler; cook over boiling water 6 minutes, or until smooth and thickened. Remove from heat; add vanilla.
- Alternately layer vanilla wafers and bananas in 9 by 9-inch or 1½-quart baking dish. Pour hot custard over layers. Let stand until cool.
- Preheat oven to 400 degrees.
- Beat egg whites until stiff but not dry. Gradually add remaining ¼ cup sugar, beating until very stiff and glossy. Spread meringue over pudding.
- Bake 10 minutes; do not overbrown. Serve warm, or cool and refrigerate until ready to serve.

Yield: 6 to 9 servings

Bread Pudding with Whiskey Sauce

1 16-ounce loaf French
bread
3 cups milk
1 cup cream sherry
3 large eggs, beaten
2 cups sugar
4 tablespoons butter,
melted, divided
2 tablespoons vanilla
extract
1 cup raisins
½ cup honey
Whiskey Sauce

• Preheat oven to 350 degrees.
• Break bread into small chunks; place in a large bowl. Add milk and sherry; soak 10 minutes. Stir until thoroughly mixed.
• Combine eggs, sugar, 2 tablespoons of the butter, and vanilla; add to bread mixture, stirring well. Stir in raisins. Spoon mixture into a lightly greased 8 by 12-inch baking dish.
• Combine the remaining 2 tablespoons butter and honey; pour over pudding.
• Bake 45 minutes, or until set. Serve with Whiskey Sauce.

Yield: 10 to 12 servings

Whiskey Sauce

¼ pound (1 stick) butter
1 cup milk
1 cup sugar
2 tablespoons cornstarch
¼ cup cold water
¾ cup bourbon

• Combine butter, milk, and sugar in a heavy saucepan; cook over low heat until butter melts and sugar dissolves.
• Combine cornstarch and water, stirring well; add to butter mixture. Add bourbon, and bring mixture to a boil over medium heat; cook 1 minute.

Yield: 2¾ cups

Cherry Walnut Pudding

1 cup sugar
1 cup flour
1 teaspoon baking soda
1 egg, beaten
1 tablespoon butter,
    melted
1 cup canned red cherries,
    drained but do not rinse
1 cup chopped nuts
Sauce

- Preheat oven to 350 degrees.
- Combine sugar, flour, and baking soda in a mixing bowl.
- In a separate bowl, combine egg and butter; add to dry ingredients. Stir in cherries and nuts. Pour into a greased 9 by 9-inch baking dish.
- Bake 35 minutes. Top with Sauce and serve warm.

Yield: 6 to 9 servings

Sauce

1 cup sugar
¼ pound (1 stick) butter
½ cup whipping cream
1 teaspoon vanilla extract

- Combine all ingredients in a heavy saucepan. Cook over low heat, stirring constantly, until thickened.

Italian Custard

1 cup sugar
1 cup cornstarch
2 quarts milk
2 teaspoons vanilla extract
2 teaspoons cinnamon or
    nutmeg

- Combine sugar and cornstarch. Add milk. Stir well and cook over medium heat until thickened.
- Remove from heat; add vanilla. Pour into 9 by 9-inch baking dish; sprinkle top with cinnamon or nutmeg. Chill until ready to serve.

Yield: 8 to 10 servings

Flan

1⅔ cups sugar, divided
4 cups milk
4 eggs
1 teaspoon vanilla extract

- Preheat oven to 400 degrees.
- Caramelize ⅔ cup of the sugar in a small pan until medium brown in color; pour this mixture into individual baking dishes.
- Combine milk and the remaining 1 cup sugar in a saucepan, stirring to mix. Simmer 5 to 6 minutes; cool.
- Beat eggs slightly to mix yolks and whites. Pour milk mixture into eggs; blend. Remove any foam. Stir in vanilla. Fill baking dishes and place in a pan of cold water.
- Bake 45 minutes. Custard is done when firm to the touch. Chill.
- When ready to serve, unmold by running knife around dish and inverting on plate. Can be made several days in advance and refrigerated.

Yield: Ten 6-ounce servings

Note: Can be poured into a 9-inch pie pan for a different look. Pretty displayed on a cake stand garnished with toasted almonds, fresh mint, or fresh berries.

Caramel Pecan Ice Cream

2 tablespoons butter
1 cup chopped pecans
½ cup sugar
4 cups half-and-half
1 cup firmly packed brown sugar
2 12-ounce jars caramel ice cream topping
1 tablespoon vanilla extract
4 cups whipping cream

- Melt butter in an 8-inch heavy skillet; add pecans and sugar. Cook over medium heat, stirring constantly, until sugar melts and turns golden brown (about 6 to 8 minutes). Drop by rounded teaspoonfuls onto wax paper; cool. Break into small clusters and set aside.

- Combine half-and-half, brown sugar, ice cream topping, and vanilla, mixing well. Stir in whipping cream and pecan clusters. Pour mixture into freezer container of 1-gallon freezer. Freeze until firm.

- After freezing, pack with additional ice and salt; let stand 1 hour to ripen.

Yield: 3 quarts

Easy Vanilla Ice Cream

2 14-ounce cans sweetened condensed milk
8 cups milk
2 tablespoons vanilla extract

- Combine all ingredients, mixing well. Pour into container of ice cream freezer; freeze until firm.

Yield: 1½ gallons

Apricot Balls

1 medium orange, juiced
  and rind grated
1 cup sugar
1 pound dried apricots,
  processed until ground
1 cup finely chopped nuts
Confectioners' sugar

- Combine orange juice and grated rind in heavy saucepan; add sugar, stirring to mix. Blend in ground apricots. Cook on preheated stovetop unit, medium heat, 10 minutes, stirring constantly.
- Add pecans; heat for 1 to 2 additional minutes, stirring constantly and mashing to combine thoroughly. Cool.
- Shape into marble-size balls; roll in confectioners' sugar, keeping hands dry with sugar.

Yield: 8 dozen

Bananas Foster

2 tablespoons butter
4 small bananas
2 tablespoons firmly
  packed brown sugar
Dash of ground cinnamon
1 tablespoon banana
  liqueur
½ cup rum
Ice cream

- Melt butter in small skillet. Cut bananas in half lengthwise; brown in butter. Sprinkle with brown sugar and cinnamon.
- Add liqueur and rum; set aflame. Serve over ice cream.

Yield: 4 servings

Apricot Pavlova

3 egg whites
1 cup sugar
2 teaspoons cornstarch
1 teaspoon vinegar

Filling

½ 15¼-ounce can apricots,
drained and chopped
1 8-ounce container frozen
whipped topping, thawed
Sliced almonds, lightly
toasted

- Preheat oven to 325 degrees.
- Beat egg whites until very stiff. Combine sugar and cornstarch. Add slowly to eggs while continuing to beat. Stir in vinegar; beat. Spread into generously greased 8 or 9-inch pie pan.
- Bake 30 minutes, or until lightly browned. Cool completely. Lift meringue out of pie pan onto serving dish.
- To prepare Filling, combine apricots and whipped topping. Spread into pie shell. Sprinkle with almonds, if desired, or remaining ½ can chopped apricots.

Yield: 6 to 8 servings

Butterfinger Trifle

1 18-ounce package
brownie mix
2 3½-ounce packages
instant chocolate
pudding
1 16-ounce container
frozen whipped topping,
thawed
6 Butterfinger candy bars,
crushed

- Bake brownies according to package directions.
- Mix pudding according to package directions.
- Crumble half of brownies into bottom of a trifle dish. Layer with ½ of pudding, ½ of crushed candy bars, and ½ of whipped topping over brownies. Repeat. Garnish with candy crumbs. Refrigerate.

Yield: 10 to 12 servings

Fresh Peach Cobbler

½ cup plus 1 tablespoon
  sugar, divided
1 tablespoon cornstarch
¼ teaspoon ground
  cinnamon
4 cups sliced peaches
  (6 medium) or 2 16-
  ounce packages frozen
  peaches
1 teaspoon lemon juice
1 cup all-purpose flour
1½ teaspoons baking
  powder
½ teaspoon salt
3 tablespoons shortening
½ cup milk
Ice cream or whipped
  cream

- Preheat oven to 400 degrees.
- Combine ½ cup of the sugar, the cornstarch, and cinnamon in 2-quart saucepan. Stir in peaches and lemon juice. Cook over medium heat, stirring constantly, until mixture thickens and boils. Boil and stir 1 minute. Pour into ungreased 2-quart baking dish; keep hot in oven.
- Combine flour, the remaining 1 tablespoon sugar, the baking powder, and salt in a medium bowl. Cut in shortening, using pastry blender or crisscrossing 2 knives, until mixture resembles fine crumbs. Stir in milk. Drop dough by spoonfuls into hot peach mixture.
- Bake 25 to 30 minutes, or until topping is golden brown. Serve with ice cream or whipped cream.

Yield: 6 servings

Kahlúa Trifle

1 18½-ounce box
chocolate cake mix with
pudding
2 3½-ounce packages
instant chocolate
pudding mix
2 cups milk
1½ cups Kahlúa, divided
2 12-ounce containers
frozen whipped topping,
thawed, divided
Chocolate morsels, pecans,
cherries, crushed toffee
for garnish, optional

• Bake cake according to
package directions for a
9 by 13-inch pan; cool on
wire rack.

• Combine pudding mixes,
milk, and ¾ cup Kahlúa;
fold in 1 container whipped
topping; chill.

• Crumble cake in a large bowl;
drizzle remaining ¾ cup
Kahlúa over cake, stirring
gently using a wooden spoon.
Layer in a trifle bowl ½ of the
cake crumbs, ½ of the pudding
mixture, and ½ of the remaining whipped topping. Repeat
layers once, ending with
whipped topping. Garnish, if
desired. Chill 8 hours.

Yield: 10 to 12 servings

*Variation: 4 tablespoons strong brewed coffee and
1 teaspoon sugar may be substituted for Kahlúa,
if desired.*

Basic Pastry

1¼ **cups all-purpose flour**
½ **teaspoon salt**
½ **cup shortening**
3 **to** 4 **tablespoons cold water**

- Combine flour and salt in medium bowl; cut in shortening with pastry blender until crumbly. Sprinkle cold water, 1 tablespoon at a time, evenly over surface; stir mixture with a fork just until dry ingredients are moistened.

- Shape dough into flattened disk; wrap in plastic wrap, and chill 2 hours or freeze 30 minutes.

- Preheat oven to 450 degrees, if a baked crust is needed.

- Roll dough out to ⅛-inch thickness on a lightly floured surface. Place in 9-inch pie plate; trim off excess pastry along edges. Fold edges under, and crimp.

- Prick bottom and sides of pastry crust generously with a fork for a baked pastry shell. (Do not prick if pastry crust is to be filled before baking.)

- Bake 10 to 12 minutes or until golden brown. Cool on wire rack.

Yield: one 9-inch pastry shell

Graham Cracker Crust

1½ cups graham cracker
crumbs (20 squares)
1 tablespoon sugar
6 tablespoons butter,
melted
¼ teaspoon vanilla extract

- Preheat oven to 350 degrees.
- Combine crumbs and sugar in small bowl. In a separate small bowl, combine butter and vanilla; mix into crumb mixture. Press into a 9-inch pieplate.
- Bake 10 minutes. Remove from oven; cool completely on wire rack.

Yield: one 9-inch shell

Basic Meringue

3 egg whites
¼ teaspoon cream of
tartar
½ teaspoon baking
powder, optional
3 tablespoons sugar
½ teaspoon vanilla extract

- Preheat oven to 400 degrees.
- In a mixing bowl, beat egg whites with cream of tartar until foamy. Add baking powder if extra-high meringue is desired. Gradually add sugar, beating until peaks are stiff and glossy. Add vanilla. Spread meringue on pie, covering to seal all edges.
- Bake 8 to 10 minutes, or until lightly browned. Remove from oven; cool on wire rack away from drafts. "Tears" form if meringue is cooled too quickly.

Yield: Meringue for 1 pie

Caramel Pie

3 egg yolks
1 cup milk
1½ cups sugar, divided
¼ pound (1 stick) butter
2 tablespoons all-purpose
   flour
1 teaspoon vanilla extract
1 9-inch pie crust, baked
   and cooled
Basic Meringue, page 300

- In a mixing bowl, combine egg yolks, milk, and 1 cup of the sugar. Set aside.
- In a heavy skillet, melt butter over medium-high heat. Add flour and stir until paste is formed. Slowly stir in egg mixture. Cook, stirring often, until thickened and smooth.
- While custard is cooking, heat the remaining ½ cup sugar in small heavy skillet over medium heat until clear and medium caramel color, being careful not to scorch.
- Remove custard from heat; slowly pour in caramelized sugar, stirring until well blended. Add vanilla and pour into prepared pie crust. Top with Basic Meringue.

Yield: one 9-inch pie

Note: Custard and caramelized sugar should be prepared at the same time so both will be very hot to blend properly.

Caramel Coconut Ice Cream Pie

1 8-ounce package cream cheese, softened
1 14-ounce can sweetened condensed milk
1 16-ounce container frozen whipped topping, thawed
4 tablespoons butter
½ cup chopped nuts
1 7-ounce can dry flaked coconut
2 9-inch pie crusts, baked and cooled
1 12-ounce jar caramel topping

- Combine cream cheese and condensed milk, mixing until smooth. Fold in whipped topping.
- Melt butter in a small heavy skillet. Stir in nuts and coconut. Sauté until lightly browned.
- Layer ¼ of the cream cheese mixture in each pie crust. Drizzle with ¼ of the caramel topping. Sprinkle with ¼ of the coconut mixture. Repeat layers, using remaining ingredients. Freeze until firm or overnight. Keep frozen until needed.

Yield: two 9-inch pies

Grape Pie

¾ cup sugar
¼ cup cornstarch
1⅓ cups grape juice
1 egg, beaten
2 tablespoons butter
2 tablespoons lemon juice
1 9-inch pie crust, baked and cooled
Whipped cream

- In a saucepan, combine sugar and cornstarch, mixing well. Gradually stir in grape juice. Cook over medium heat until mixture is smooth and has thickened.
- Remove from heat; stir mixture slowly into beaten egg. Return to heat and cook 1 minute.
- Remove from heat; stir in butter and lemon juice. Pour into pie crust. Chill until set. Serve with whipped cream.

Yield: one 9-inch pie

Coconut Pie

⅓ cup all-purpose flour or
¼ cup cornstarch
¾ cup sugar
¼ teaspoon salt
2 cups milk
3 egg yolks, slightly
beaten
2 tablespoons butter
1 teaspoon vanilla extract
1 cup coconut plus
additional for garnish
1 9-inch pie crust, baked

Meringue

3 egg whites
½ teaspoon baking
powder
½ cup sugar

- Preheat oven to 350 degrees.
- Combine flour or cornstarch, sugar, and salt; gradually add milk. Cook over moderate heat, stirring constantly until mixture thickens and boils. Cook an additional 2 minutes; remove from heat.
- Add small amount of cooked mixture to egg yolks; stir into remaining hot mixture. Cook 1 minute. Add butter, vanilla, and coconut; cool slightly. Pour into pie crust.
- To prepare Meringue, beat egg whites and baking powder until stiff. Add sugar and blend well. Cover pie with Meringue, making sure to seal all edges or pie will weep. Sprinkle with additional coconut.
- Bake 15 minutes.

Yield: one 9-inch pie crust

Variation: Pineapple pie: Add 1 cup well-drained crushed pineapple.

Chocolate pie: Add 2 squares unsweetened melted chocolate or 3 tablespoons cocoa mixed with a small amount of water to make a thick paste. Paste must be fairly thick, or pie will be runny.

Banana pie: Slice 3 bananas in bottom of crust; add filling.

Caramel pie: Caramelize ¼ cup of the sugar. Gradually add scalded milk, mixing well.

Omit coconut for variations.

Ice Cream Pie

**16 graham cracker
squares, crushed**
1½ cups sugar, divided
1 teaspoon cinnamon
**6 tablespoons butter,
melted**
**1 12-ounce can evaporated
milk, chilled**
2½ lemons, juiced
**1 8-ounce can crushed
pineapple, drained and
excess moisture
squeezed out**
½ banana, mashed

- Preheat oven to 350 degrees.
- Combine cracker crumbs,
½ cup of the sugar, and
cinnamon in small bowl.
Add butter; mix into crumbled
mixture. Press into 10-inch
pie pan. Bake 10 minutes.
Remove from oven; cool
completely.
- In a small mixing bowl, beat
milk on high speed with
chilled beaters until thick.
Gradually add the remaining
1 cup sugar and lemon juice,
beating until thickened. Stir in
pineapple and banana.
- Pour into prepared pie crust;
freeze for several hours or
overnight.

Yield: one 10-inch pie

*Note: May add a drop of food coloring for special holidays or to
enhance china.*

Chocolate Chess Pie

1½ cups sugar
**¼ pound (1 stick) butter,
melted**
3½ tablespoons cocoa
2 eggs, beaten
1 teaspoon vanilla extract
**1 5-ounce can evaporated
milk**
1 9-inch pie crust, unbaked

- Preheat oven to 325 degrees.
- Combine sugar, butter, cocoa,
eggs, vanilla, and evaporated
milk, mixing well on low
setting of mixer. Pour into
pie crust.
- Bake 45 minutes, or until set.

Yield: one 9-inch pie

Pecan Pie

1 cup chopped or whole
pecans
1 9-inch pie crust, unbaked
3 eggs
1 cup corn syrup
½ cup sugar
4 tablespoons butter,
melted
1 teaspoon vanilla extract
Dash of salt

• Preheat oven to 275 degrees.
• Place pecans in bottom of pie crust.
• In a mixing bowl, beat eggs slightly; add corn syrup, sugar, butter, vanilla, and salt, mixing well to combine. Pour into pie crust over pecans.
• Bake 35 minutes. Increase heat to 300 degrees; bake an additional 20 minutes, or until set.

Yield: one 9-inch pie

Old-Fashioned Lemon Pie

3 eggs, separated
1 cup plus 1 tablespoon
sugar, divided
3 tablespoons cornstarch
1½ cups water
1 tablespoon butter,
melted and cooled
2 lemons, juiced and rind
grated
1 9-inch pie crust, baked
and cooled
¼ teaspoon cream of tartar

• Preheat oven to 400 degrees.
• Beat egg yolks slightly in a small bowl.
• In top of double boiler, combine 1 cup of the sugar, the cornstarch, water, butter, lemon juice, grated rind, and beaten egg; cook over medium heat until thickened, stirring often. Pour into prepared crust.
• In a small mixing bowl, combine egg whites and cream of tartar, beating until frothy. Add the remaining 1 tablespoon sugar; beat until stiff, glossy peaks form. Spread on top of pie, sealing all edges.
• Bake 8 to 10 minutes, or until lightly browned.

Yield: one 9-inch pie

Contributors...

The **Pick of the Crop, Two** committee would like to express our appreciation to everyone who contributed their favorite recipes, without which, this cookbook would not have been possible. We also thank those who spent hours testing and tasting the recipes. Our deepest gratitude goes to all those listed here and to anyone we may have inadvertently failed to mention. We regret that we were unable to include all recipes submitted due to similarity or availability of space.

Contributors, Testers, and Student Helpers

Jane Allen
Twyla Allen
Donna Allred
Timmy Allred
Penny Andrews
Ann Elizabeth Arant
Kathryn Arant
Lucy Arant
Miriam Atkinson
Lee Aylwood
Jan Barr
Georgia Baughman
Lucille Baughman
Mrs. Theo D. Bennett
Wanda Belk
Jean Bernardi
Jeff Blackmun
Georgia Blackwell
Jennifer Blackwood
Valrie Blackwood
Mary Jane Blakeman
Vicki Bledsoe
Bettie Borgonelli
Margie Bowen
Judy Bowman
Susan Bowman
Katherine Braswell
DeAngela Brenza
Jay Brenza
Maureen Brooks
Pam Brooks
Barry Bryant
Kathy Bryant
Suzanne Burch
Hudean Burkhalter
Sally Burnett
Betty Burrell
Chelle Chandler

Mary Jane Chandler
Sheba Chandler
Sheila Chandler
Carly Clark
Frony Clark
Sheila Clark
Linda Cobb
Bonnie Cole
LaBreska Cole
Maurine Cole
Ella Craft
Wilma Culp
Brenda Cummins
Kathy Cummins
Wanda Cummins
Billy Curbow
Dekoka Davidson
June Davis
Bobby Day
Jane Dickerson
Kathy Dickerson
Drew Dickerson
Sister Dorrough
Bobbie DuBard
Jane Dunlap
Arie Earls
Marilyn East
Carolyn Eastland
Barbara Edwards
Lina Elfert
Lucy Elfert
Freida Ellis
Somer Erwin
Bobbie Estes
Pam Eubanks
Wade Eubanks
Christin Faulkner
Terri Flanagan

Pam Fleming
Paulette Fleming
Winnie Flemmons
Kenneth W. Ford
Ann Francis
Blanche S. Francis
Janice Fullen
Wynell Farrish
Katherine Garrett
Jan Garrison
Nancy Gee
Jimmy George
Janet Godwin
Mandy Gray
Allan Grittman
Ann Grittman
Belle Grittman
Cindy Grittman
Robin West Grubb
Ella Guest
Janet Harmon
Lona Skeen Harris
Cyndie Tollison Harrison
Tom Harrison
Mary Harvey
Michelle Herring
Nikki Kyle Herring
Charlotte Hill
Fay Hill
Amanda Holder
Pam Posey Holder
Henrietta Holeman
Ann Smaltz Holladay
Susan Crow Hollinger
Charles Wesley Holmes
Rebecca White Hood
Cindy Horton
Myra Hughes
Jo Beth Janoush
Claude Johnson
Joy Starnes Jones
Lynn Jones
Missy LaMastus Kapaun
Eschol Kea
Cedie Kendall
Lance Kimbrell
Rossie King
Carol Kyle
Courtney Kyle

Nancy Kyle
Diddy LaMastus
Allyson Arant Land
John Phillip Land
Margaret Land
Sue Latham
Barbara Levingston
Allison Lienard
Rich Lienard
Sarah Love
Will Love
Sandra Manning
Sis Manning
Katherine Ann Marlow
Vera Alice Marlow
Pinkie Maxwell
Tem Mayfield
Diane McCreary
Ann McClure
Hazel McCool
Melissa McKellar
Jenny Ellis McNeer
Ramona Kyle McShan
Barry McWilliams
Jack McWilliams
Johnny McWilliams
Bea Meador
Nena Melton
Ann Milam
Anne Milburn
Dotty Miller
Emily Miller
Mabel Miller
Ruth Miller
Tucker Miller
Hayes Mitchell
Lloyd Mitchell
L. E. Moon
Carol Moore
Jennifer Moore
Pat Moore
Betty Murphey
Shirley Neal
Stephanie Neal
Maxine Nelson
Angel Nickens
Barbara Nielson
Kristi Nielson
Bert Oakes

Janet Oakes
Lucille Oakes
Jackie Orsborn
Laura Orsborn
Cyndi Owen
Shurden Owen
Vicky Parish
Dianne Parker
Tina Lasyone Parker
Glenda Parks
Gloria Pedersen
Francis Pentecost
Vicki Pentecost
Annie Mae Petrie
Rita Pitts
Doll Posey
Wanda Prince
Kathryn Purcell
Monica Raney
Vallie Ray
Mary Reese
Mrs. William G. Reymond
Teresa Reynolds
Michelle Richardson
Cherri Rickels
Clara Belle Robertson
Mrs. Jerry Robinson
Amber Russell
Mandy Russell
Debbie Sanders
Anthony Seta
Pam Manning Shelton
Frances Showers
Diane Shurden
Steve Shurden
Genice Shurden
Joy Springer
Peggy Stainback
Zil Stansel
Mandy Steelman
JoAnne Story
Tammy Braswell Story
Carol Tatum
Betty Templeton
Beverly Terrell
Imogene Terrell
Melanie Terrell
Electra Thomas
Jason Thompson

Mary Thompson
Jeri LaMastus Thompson
Ann Parker Thorn
Marie Threet
Nancy Tidmore
Sheila Tolbert
Merle Tolbert
Ansley Tollison
Becky Tollison
Bubba Tollison
Lillian Trahan
Kathy Tribble
Eleanor Trimble
Erin Turpin
Shelby Ulrey
Mitzi Moody Vance
Brenda Vanlandingham
Monica Vanlandingham
Eloise Walker
Alisha Walls
Christal Walls
Shirley Walters
Lyle Ward
Pat Ward
Kathy Warfield
Blanche Watkins
Kathy Weaver
Erica Weed
Debbie Weeks
Donnie West
Gwendolyn West
Russell West
Nell Westbrook
Dee Williams
Louise Williams
Mary Agnes Williams
Sarah Williams
Carmon Willingham
Cindy Willingham
Darlene Willingham
Ollie Sue Willingham
Andrea Wilson
Wynn Windham
Kelly Woods
Don Yates
Doris Yates
Helen Young
Hope Young

Index

INDEX

INDEX

INDEX

INDEX

INDEX

INDEX

INDEX

Pick of the Crop, Two ORDER FORM

Name _____

Address _____

City _____ State _____ Zip _____

Phone _____

Send check or money order payable to:
Pick of the Crop, Two
148 Academy Road • Drew, MS 38737
601-756-0088
800-208-4098

Please do not send cash. Sorry, no C.O.D.'s.
Visa and MasterCard accepted.

ISBN #0-9666954-0-2

Item	Qty.	Unit	Total
Pick of the Crop, Two Cookbook		$18.95	
		Subtotal	$
	Applicable MS Sales Tax (residents only):		$
	Shipping/Handling ($4.00 each book)		$
		Total enclosed	$

Pick of the Crop, Two ORDER FORM

Name _____

Address _____

City _____ State _____ Zip _____

Phone _____

Send check or money order payable to:
Pick of the Crop, Two
148 Academy Road • Drew, MS 38737
601-756-0088
800-208-4098

Please do not send cash. Sorry, no C.O.D.'s.
Visa and MasterCard accepted.

ISBN #0-9666954-0-2

Item	Qty.	Unit	Total
Pick of the Crop, Two Cookbook		$18.95	
		Subtotal	$
	Applicable MS Sales Tax (residents only):		$
	Shipping/Handling ($4.00 each book)		$
		Total enclosed	$

Additional Prints

Additional prints of the cover art of the **Pick of the Crop, Two** may be ordered from:

Mrs. Barry McWilliams
141 South Third Street
Drew, MS 38737

	Amount
Send me _____ 8"x10" signed and numbered color print(s) of cookbook cover art @ $12.50 a print.	_____
Send me _____ set(s) of 5 - 4"x6" cottonboll color notecards w/envelopes @ $8.50 a set.	_____
Please add $1.50 for postage and handling.	1.50
MS residents add 7% sales tax.	_____
Total	_____

Name _____

Address _____

City _____ State _____ Zip _____